OUTLAW TALES
of New Mexico

OUTLAW TALES
of New Mexico

True Stories of New Mexico's Most Infamous Robbers, Rustlers, and Bandits

Barbara Marriott

TWODOT®

GUILFORD, CONNECTICUT
HELENA, MONTANA
AN IMPRINT OF THE GLOBE PEQUOT PRESS

To buy books in quantity for corporate use
or incentives, call **(800) 962–0973**
or e-mail **premiums@GlobePequot.com.**

A · T W O D O T® · B O O K

Map by M. A. Dubé © Morris Book Publishing, LLC.

Library of Congress Cataloging-in-Publication Data is available.
ISBN 978-0-7627-4320-9

Manufactured in the United States of America
First Edition/First Printing

The story of our society and our culture would be lost if it were not for the many museums, libraries, and historical societies whose volunteers and professional archivists work tirelessly to preserve our national history. Because of them we know who we were and who we are, and we have a fair idea of who we will become. We owe them a debt of gratitude, and this book is dedicated to them.

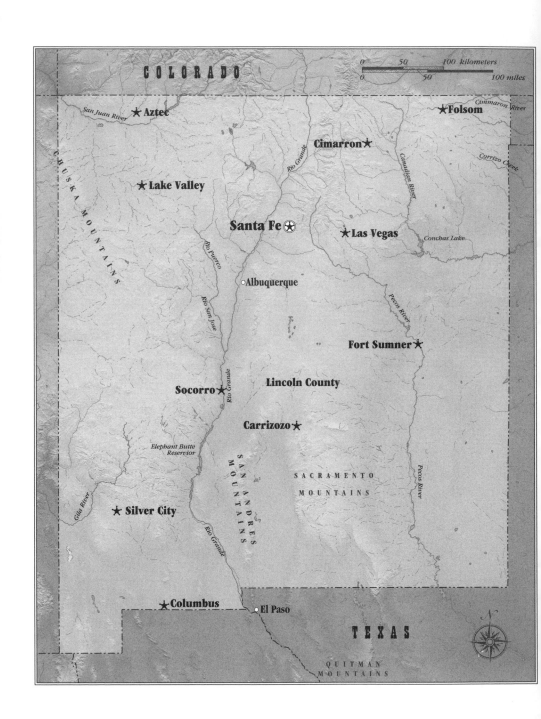

COLORADO

0   50   100 kilometers
0   50   100 miles

★ Aztec

San Juan River

Cimarron ★

★Folsom

Cimmaron River

Corrizo Creek

Rio Grande

Canadian River

★ Lake Valley

CHUSKA MOUNTAINS

Santa Fe ✪

★ Las Vegas

Conchas Lake

Rio Puerco

Albuquerque

Rio San Jose

Pecos River

Fort Sumner ★

Socorro ★

Rio Grande

Lincoln County

Carrizozo ★

Elephant Butte
Reservior

SAN ANDRES MOUNTAINS

SACRAMENTO

MOUNTAINS

Pecos River

Gila River

★ Silver City

Rio Grande

★ Columbus

El Paso

TEXAS

QUITMAN
MOUNTAINS

NEW MEXICO

Contents

Acknowledgments

This book is dedicated to all the archivists and volunteers who did their best to find unknown photographs and written documents for this book. Very special thanks go to Donald Burge at the Center for Southwest Research in Albuquerque, New Mexico, for all of his help. Thanks also go to Sibel Melik at the New Mexico State Records Center and Archives; Natalia Sciarini at the Beinecke Rare Book and Manuscript Library; Daniel Kosharek, photo archivist, and the rest of the staff at the Palace of the Governors; the New Mexico History Museum; Tomas Jaehn and volunteer archivist Kathryn Robens at the Fra Angelico Chavez Library; and the Museum of New Mexico. Thank you to Joe Sabatini, manager of the Special Collections Library at the City of Albuquerque Library, and to LaVern Robinson, executive secretary at the Socorro County Chamber of Commerce. Thanks to Kathy Weiser of www.legendsofamerica.com for the picture of Dirty Dave Rudabaugh's head, and also to Susanne Smith for providing assorted images. This book could not have come together without the abundant help of these hardworking people.

Introduction

They rode across the land with their six-shooters and rifles blazing. They were courageous, they were cowardly; they were the law, and they were the lawless. Collectively, they became an icon of the Old West. It's been more than a hundred years since the days of the western outlaws, but their evil deeds and adventures still fascinate us. Maybe what grabs our interest is the sheer variety of their deeds and personalities—forming a veritable smorgasbord of badness and derring-do.

There were clever outlaws, like Vincent Silva, who fooled a town, and a few stupid ones, like Milton Yarberry, who used his six-gun instead of his brains.

Billy the Kid, perhaps the most famous of the western outlaws, entices us with his charismatic personality, while Joel Fowler, a biter and a fighter, was liked by hardly anyone. The righteous Clay Allison "never killed a man who didn't need killing," while the pathetic, passionate Ada Hulmes killed only for revenge. A few walked the line between law and lawlessness, sometimes acting as lawman, other times as outlaw.

The outlaws came to their rough ways by different routes. The road for some was a trip through the violence of a war that took their homes and their families. Others turned to thieving because they walked a path of hardship. And some were just born nasty.

However they got there, the characters profiled in this book all wound up riding the lawless trail. Most of them ended their journey by being hanged or shot; a few lucky ones simply disappeared.

The New Mexico Territory was a land born in nature's violence. The deep canyons, grassy plains, undulating horizons, and sky islands called to men and women who wanted a new life. They came and established cattle ranches, businesses, and mining towns. But only the rugged could survive in this wild land. The soil was poor for farming; the mountains cut jagged slices into the land, and the only way you could keep good rangeland was to fight for it.

Among those who came to the New Mexico Territory were bad men, outlaws, desperados, and disreputable folk. The law in this land was inconsistent, corrupt, or nonexistent, and the rugged landscape offered sanctuary for many men and women on the run. Fledgling towns sometimes supplied money and fame for good shooters. Jobs were available, and no questions were asked about a man or a woman's past.

A dozen outlaws are profiled on the pages that follow. You may not understand all of their motivations, and you may not care for their deeds—but like 'em or not, they defined the Old West and helped create much of its history.

Robert "Clay" Allison
A Legend Made of Tall Tales, Myths, and Downright Lies

Red River, New Mexico, was a tiny settlement in the middle of nowhere. It consisted of a few buildings; one was a hotel called the Clifton House. The Clifton House was a grand three-story hotel with an especially fine restaurant.

Besides the Clifton House, Red River had one other attraction. And this one brought cattlemen and horsemen to town from near and far. Behind the hotel was a quarter-mile racetrack. Owners would bring in their fastest horses for informal match races run 'round the track. While there was nothing professional about these races, they were taken quite seriously.

On the evening of January 7, 1874, in this nowhere town, two men sat facing each other over dinner in a small, dimly lit chili parlor across from the Clifton House. The scene looked normal enough—except there was a feeling of expectation, distrust, and danger hanging in the air.

One of the diners, Clay Allison, had left his Cimarron ranch earlier that day with his favorite racing horse. He headed for Red River planning a day at the races and what he believed would be a big win. What he didn't plan on was meeting a familiar face—that of Chuck Colbert.

Colbert was considered to be one of the baddest outlaws in the West. He was credited with killing more than seven men, and he wanted to add Allison to the list. His reasons were both personal and professional. Allison was considered a pure "shootist," a man respected for his talent with a gun—and that made him a good target for a man trying to widen his reputation as a gunslinger. That was Colbert's professional reason.

1

Colbert's personal reason had to do with his Uncle Zack Colbert. Uncle Zack had been a ferryman on the Red River near Denison, Texas, when Allison and his family headed west from Tennessee after the Civil War. Seems Allison didn't like the price of crossing, so he beat or killed Uncle Zack, then proceeded to ferry his family across the river for nothing. Colbert never forgot or forgave the incident.

The races for the day were over when Colbert challenged Allison's champion. Their steeds went head to head, and the race ended in a dead heat. Neither Colbert nor Allison was happy with the results, and their behavior toward each other was like a lukewarm blanket over a sheet of ice.

Trying to put up a front of good sportsmanship, they agreed to have dinner together, but not before they shared a few more drinks—and both had already been tipping the bottle much of the day. Colbert's friend Charles Cooper joined them at a table, and Colbert and Allison sat down across from each other.

When dinner was over, the men sat sipping their coffee. Colbert, a right-hander, slowly reached for his coffee with his left hand. Allison noticed the unusual move. His sharp reflexes clicked in, and his chair crashed to the floor as he leaned backwards just as Colbert's right hand went to his lap and came away with his six-shooter. Colbert rushed his shot, and the bullet plowed into the table. He didn't get a second chance. Allison whipped his gun up and shot Colbert in the face, driving the bullet home above his right eye and ending the life of the killer gunman. Allison felt no remorse; he believed that Colbert intended to kill him.

Twelve days later, Cooper, who had shared that ill-fated dinner with Colbert and Allison, was seen riding toward Cimarron. After that he completely disappeared. Talk was that Allison had killed him. It took two years for the authorities to charge Allison with Cooper's murder, but no proof could be found, and Allison was released.

Speculation about the murder of Cooper was just one of the many rumors, myths, and half-truths that surround Clay Allison. For example, take his physique. He was listed by the army as being five feet eleven,

Clay Allison at twenty-six

Courtesy Western History Collection, University of Oklahoma Library, Rose Collection, #2143

but others had him at six feet to six feet two inches. He was reported to have shiny hazel-brown eyes by a resident of Cimarron, but clear blue eyes by others. And his decided limp? It was attributed to his being born with a clubfoot. But it was also attributed to his having shot himself through the instep of his right foot as an adult. Perhaps he shot himself through his clubfoot.

And then there were his escapades in the Civil War. Allison bragged that he served as a scout for General Nathan Bedford Forrest, was captured, declared a spy, and sentenced to death. He told of escaping on the eve he was to be shot as a spy by the Yankee guards. As Allison told it, he got away by swimming ashore from Johnson Island, Ohio, in Lake Erie's Sandusky Bay. But there is some confusion between the story Allison told and the official Confederate Army records—which list Allison as being a prisoner in Alabama from May 4 through May 10, 1865.

Allison's life as a youngster was simpler and more peaceful than his life as an adult. Things started out good for the Allison family. Clay was born in Wayne County, Tennessee, on September 2, 1841. He was the fourth child in a family of eight children, and his father was a Presbyterian circuit rider.

Allison was living on his family farm when the Civil War broke out. He left home and joined the Tennessee Light Artillery. But three months later he was back on the farm with a medical discharge. The army doctors reported that Allison was "incapable of performing the duties of a soldier because of a blow received many years ago. Emotional or physical excitement produces paroxysmals of a mixed character, partly epileptic and partly maniacal."

His civilian life didn't last long. Clay was determined to fight the Yankee aggressors. He reenlisted, this time in Company F, Nineteenth Tennessee Cavalry. He served two years, until the regiment surrendered on May 4, 1865. He took away from the war a deep and abiding hatred for Yankees, blacks, and soldiers in particular.

Clay was home from the army one day when a corporal from the Third Illinois Cavalry rode up to the farmhouse. The corporal announced he was going to take all the household valuables. In his enthusiasm the corporal picked up, then accidentally dropped, Mrs. Allison's prized pitcher. Allison went to the closet, pulled out his gun, and killed the soldier.

It was this unpredictable behavior that marked Allison as a dangerous man and led to the web of dark fantasies woven around him. Ordinarily a quiet and polite man, Allison could explode with an unreasonable and violent rage at the slightest provocation. Drinking seemed to trigger his unbalanced mental condition.

In the late 1860s Allison was hired as a cowboy for cattle drivers Charles Goodnight and Oliver Loving. He accompanied the drive that went from Fort Belknap, Texas, to the Pecos River, then to Fort Sumner in the New Mexico Territory, and finally on to Denver in the Colorado Territory. It was on that drive that Clay first saw New Mexico and decided to someday make the land his home.

And the opportunity soon arose. His brother-in-law, Lew Coleman, and his partner, Irvin W. Lacy, decided to move their cattle operation to New Mexico Territory, and they hired Allison to head up the cattle drive. Allison was given a portion of the herd for pay, and with the cattle he earned, he was able to set up his own ranch in the Cimarron area. But while he was still on the drive, Allison couldn't control his maniacal nature. As the drive neared Cimarron City, Allison spotted a number of army mules corralled for the night. His hatred of all things army prompted him to stampede the mules.

In Cimarron, Allison's new home, his legend flourished. One day in October 1870, Clay and his friend Davy Crockett (not the Alamo Crockett) were spending the day drinking in John Pearson's saloon in Elizabethtown, New Mexico Territory, when a hysterical woman rushed in. Dulcinia Madonado Kennedy told a tale of horror. Her husband had murdered her baby son and had killed a number of travelers. She claimed he had buried the bodies under their cabin. Allison and a group of men went to the cabin where they found Kennedy too drunk to explain himself. He was arrested and placed in jail to await trial.

According to legend, Allison was furious. He believed Kennedy to be guilty of these heinous crimes, and he wanted swift justice. Judge Benjamin Houx ordered a search of the Kennedy grounds. Bones were found, but before it could be determined if the bones were human or animal, Allison and others decided to take matters into their own hands.

Kennedy was dragged from jail, taken to the local slaughterhouse, and hanged on October 7. Allison continued the assault on the dead body by picking up a butcher knife and chopping off Kennedy's head. Later, Allison and Crockett entered Henry Lambert's saloon in Cimarron with a bloody gunnysack containing the dismembered head. Allison insisted the head be displayed on a pike outside the saloon. He wanted all to know that Kennedy had been made to pay for his crimes.

The *New Mexican* published an article that had some points of disagreement with this tale. It reported that in September, Kennedy was arrested on a charge of murder. A witness testified that he saw Kennedy shoot an American while he was sleeping in the Kennedy cabin. A jury failed to reach a verdict in the case, and another trial was ordered. Meanwhile, Kennedy was placed in a secured log house for the night. Vigilantes surprised the guards, took Kennedy to the slaughterhouse, and hanged him. There is no mention of a decapitation in the story, and the fact is that the Lambert saloon was not built until two years after Kennedy was murdered. Ultimately, there is no proof that Allison was part of the vigilante mob that hanged Kennedy.

Some of the tales about Allison are more concrete. During the 1870s he killed or helped kill several men. And by 1875 he was embroiled in the "Colfax County War," a bloody land-rights dispute, setting himself on the side of homesteaders and against the Santa Fe Ring, a collective of attorneys, businessmen, and public officials bent on unscrupulously acquiring Spanish and Mexican land grants that carried over to the

United States after the Mexican War. Members of the Ring included congressional delegate Stephen Benton Elkins, U.S. District Attorney Thomas Catron, Chief Justice Joseph G. Palen, Henry L. Waldo, and County Probate Judge Robert H. Longwill.

Allison's friend Rev. F. J. Tolby was an outspoken critic of the Santa Fe Ring. On September 14, 1875, he was shot and killed returning from a visit to Elizabethtown. Cruz Vegas was arrested for the murder, but he insisted Manuel Cardenas was the guilty man. Cruz was "rescued" from the jail by a mob and hanged. Allison is reported to have shot him in the back to put him out of his misery, then cut him down, and dragged him through the desert, where his body was left to rot.

Vegas's employer, Pancho Griego, came looking for Allison. It was rumored that Griego was an enforcer for the ring. Allison and Griego met in front of the St. James Hotel. They decided to talk things out over a drink and went into the bar. Their conversation was friendly, and Griego asked Allison to step into the corner to continue their talk. They talked for a few more moments—then Allison drew his revolver and shot Griego three times. This final display of Allison's violence and instability was too much for the residents of Cimarron. The local newspaper started a campaign to get Allison removed from the area. In retaliation, Allison broke into the Cimarron *News and Press* one evening, dumped the printing press into the river, and scattered the cases of type.

The next day, Mrs. Ada Morley, owner and publisher of the newspaper, was in tears when she discovered her wrecked office. When Allison discovered the newspaper was owned by a woman, he left his ranch and rode into town to find her. Finding Morley in the destroyed office, he inquired if she were the owner. When she confirmed that she was, an embarrassed Allison reached into his shirt, pulled out a thick wad of bills, and thrust the money into her hands, telling her to buy a new press. "I don't fight women," he declared.

Clay Allison became Mrs. Morley's defending knight. When an enemy accused her of the bogus charge of stealing a registered letter and indicted her for robbing the mails, Allison sent out a warning: "Bring that woman to trial and not a man will come out of the court-room alive." No action was taken against Ada Morley.

Some tales about Allison, like this one, lend a note of humor to the lifestyle of the gunman. A shootout to the death between Allison and Mace Bowman ended with the men drinking together and then deciding who deserved the gunman's crown by stripping to their underwear and shooting at each other's feet. The dancing duel ended when both reached the point of exhaustion. And the fact that both men left the duel unscathed doesn't say much for their so-called shooting expertise. Another time, Allison reportedly raced through town bellowing a rebel yell while wearing nothing but his boots.

Yet another naked encounter was planned between Clay and a Colfax County neighbor. To settle a disagreement, they agreed to dig a grave, jump in naked, and fight with knives to the death. A blank grave-stone was placed by the pit, and the winner was to bear the responsibility of burying the dead man and having the stone properly engraved. Some say this fight happened, and Allison emerged the winner. Some say Allison died before the fight could take place. Whichever way it happened, it's all part of the Allison myth.

Allison also had serious run-ins with the law; one in particular was documented in the newspapers. Clay and his brother John were enjoying the nightlife in Las Animas, Colorado Territory, drinking and dancing at the Olympia Dance Hall. Some of the patrons complained to Sheriff Faber that the brothers were creating a disturbance, stepping on patrons' toes and trying to start fights. Faber made a weak attempt to arrest the brothers, but since they were both wearing pistols, he left the dance hall without pressing the issue.

He returned with two deputies, rifle in hand. As the lawmen entered, someone shouted, "Look out!" and Faber fired, hitting John Allison. Clay pulled his pistol out and fired at Faber, whose gun discharged as he fell to the floor, again striking John. The deputies disappeared out the door on a run. Clay followed to the front steps of the Olympic, firing at the fleeing men.

Returning to the dance hall, he dragged the dead body of Faber over to his injured brother, saying, "John, here's the man that shot you. Look at the damned son of a bitch—I killed him." Clay took John to their hotel room at the Vandiver House, and it was there that Sheriff Spires found and arrested them for the murder of Sheriff Faber. John was in serious condition, and it was believed he might not recover. Meanwhile, Allison was released on $10,000 bail on January 8, 1877. In February, John was still recovering when he was released for lack of evidence. And in March a grand jury delivered a verdict of self-defense in Allison's trial.

Clay Allison moved back to Texas in 1880 and the following year married Dora McCullough, the sister of John Allison's wife. The marriage had a sobering effect on Clay; the birth of his daughter in 1885, even more so.

But Clay had one more story up his sleeve. It is said that in the following year on a cattle trip to Wyoming, he developed a severe toothache and stopped by a dentist in Cheyenne. Unfortunately, the nervous dentist worked on the wrong tooth. An angry and still hurting Allison stormed out of the dental office. He found another dentist in town who fixed the tooth and advised Clay that he had seen a quack.

A furious Clay Allison returned to the first dentist and, seizing a pair of forceps, pulled out one of his teeth. The blood-curdling yells coming from the dentist's office brought in the townspeople just as Clay had locked onto another tooth and part of the dentist's lip. The *Las Vegas Optic* enjoyed reporting the incident, declaring the story to be true and verified by Allison himself.

Early in the month of July 1887, Clay Allison took a trip to Pecos, Texas, to buy supplies. No one knows exactly what happened on the way home, but the most likely scenario is that the load in his wagon shifted and Allison reached over to fix it, losing his balance and falling under the wagon. What we do know is that a wheel passed over his neck, breaking it and killing him. Even in the matter of death, the truth of what happened to Allison remains veiled.

Clay Allison, the dangerous gunman, died alone in a wagon accident. Engraved on his tombstone are the following words: HE NEVER KILLED A MAN THAT DID NOT NEED KILLING.

Jesse Evans

The Escape Artist

For Jesse Evans, trouble was a family affair. Born in Missouri in 1853, Evans moved to Kansas in 1871 with his family. And on June 2 of that year, the members of the Evans family were arrested for passing counterfeit money. Some went to jail, but Jesse was lucky—he was fined $500 and released. On his own, he left Kansas, stayed briefly in Texas, then crossed the border into New Mexico Territory.

Evans signed on as a wrangler for cattle baron John Chisum and worked his way up to the position of foreman. It was while he was working for Chisum that he met Billy the Kid, who would become an icon of the western outlaw. Both Billy and Evans left Chisum's employ at about the same time. Evans and his gang members, known as the "boys"—Tom Hill, Frank Rivers, and Frank Baker—began working for J. J. Dolan and L. G. Murphy, supplying stolen cattle for their government contracts. Dolan and Murphy were cattle brokers and partners in one of the town's mercantile stores. Much to their dismay, a new mercantile store had been opened by Englishman John Tunstall and Scotsman Alexander McSween, newcomers to town. Tunstall also owned a ranch, and Billy the Kid went to work for him as a wrangler. Tunstall and McSween became the bitter enemies of Dolan and Murphy, and that rivalry put Billy and Evans in opposite camps.

On New Year's Day of 1876, Evans got into serious trouble when the men he was celebrating with decided to shoot up the local dance hall in Mescilla. Their indiscriminate shots killed three soldiers from the 8th Cavalry stationed at Fort Selden. Despite the level of violence involved, no warrants were issued.

Eighteen days later, Evans was involved in another killing. Evans, Samuel Blanton, and a man named Morris were at a saloon in Las Cruces where they met Quirino Fletcher. Fletcher bragged about having killed some Texans in Chihuahua, Mexico. The idea of this Mexican killing Texans was more than the trio could tolerate. In a fit of anger, they took justice into their own hands and killed Fletcher, leaving his body in the street. The corpse lay untouched until sunrise the next morning, when Fletcher's family arrived and claimed it. Evans pleaded not guilty to the charge of murder and was ultimately acquitted.

In 1877 Evans's cattle rustling came to the attention of Albert J. Fountain, a local cattleman and political activist, who was trying to uncover proof of a connection between rustling in the Lincoln area and the Santa Fe Ring. On July 18 Fountain departed the courthouse with warrants for the arrest of Evans and several prominent citizens. After leaving the courthouse, Fountain started for home with his young son. Father and son disappeared along the route and were never seen or heard from again. Evans was suspected in the disappearance, but there was no evidence to tie him to the event. Nonetheless, he was quickly building a reputation as a man with a gun for hire—a dangerous gun.

That summer in 1877, Evans and the boys kept busy rustling livestock from several Lincoln County ranches. On one raid they took Tunstall's horses. When Tunstall found his livestock in Evans's care, he swore out a warrant for Evans's arrest. However, Sheriff Brady, a man who unofficially worked for Dolan, did nothing to serve the warrant. Tunstall's foreman took matters into his own hands. Forming a posse, he tracked down Evans and his boys and captured them. This time, Sheriff Brady had no choice but to lock up the outlaws.

In jail Evans bragged to the other prisoners that they would not hold him long. Tunstall agreed with Evans. He described the pathetic conditions of the jail, saying that the shackles were filed, the log walls had holes, and no attempt was being made to secure the prisoners. On the

Main Street of Lincoln, New Mexico, where the Lincoln County War was fought
Courtesy Palace of the Governors (MNM/DCA), #105473

night of November 16, Evans, Frank Baker, and Tom Hill walked out of the Lincoln County jail and went back to work for Dolan. No one was surprised.

On February 18, 1878, Dolan sent Evans and his boys on an errand. Dolan claimed that Tunstall owed him money, and he placed an attachment on Tunstall's property. A group of horses that had been stolen by Evans and his gang and then rescued by Tunstall were initially excluded from the attachment. However, Sheriff Brady received a new set of orders, presumably from Dolan, to get the horses. Hearing that Tunstall was driving the horses to his ranch from a holding site, Brady organized a posse to collect the horses, deputized John Matthews to lead it, and included Evans and his boys in the posse.

Jesse Evans and two of the boys rode ahead of the twenty-man posse. It was a clear, crisp February afternoon, and the trail of Tunstall's horses was easy to follow. Tunstall had gathered his small herd and, along with Billy the Kid, Robert Widenmann, Dick Brewer, and John Middleton, set out for his ranch. Billy and Middleton trailed the horses. Tunstall led the small drive with Widenmann and Brewer taking care of the middle. When the procession flushed some wild turkey, Tunstall told his hands to go after them while he waited with the herd. That's where Evans found him.

Evans, Tom Hill, and William Morton crested the ridge and saw John Tunstall and his horses, all alone, at the bottom of the canyon. "We're not going to hurt you, Tunstall," shouted Evans.

Tunstall rode toward the three men. They threw up their guns, resting their rifles on their knees, waiting for Tunstall.

"Not yet," Evans whispered, "wait until he gets nearer."

As Tunstall rode closer, Morton brought his rifle to his shoulder and fired. The bullet hit Tunstall in the chest. As he pitched forward, Evans moved toward the fallen Tunstall, retrieved his revolver, and shot him in the head. It took all three of them to load Tunstall's body on the back of his horse. Leading the horse, they moved about a hundred yards away from the trail into the trees. Morton and Hill dumped the body on the ground. Turning toward Tunstall's horse, one of them pumped a bullet into the animal's head, killing it instantly. The only eulogy they offered was, "that ought to teach the sidewinder not to buck Murphy and Dolan."

When the rest of the posse arrived, Evans explained that Tunstall's killing was an act of self-defense; Tunstall had gone for his gun when he spotted them. Some of the riders quietly questioned that story, but they turned their horses and headed back to town. Later, other members of the posse told a story of being too far back to see anything. The self-defense proclamation stood, mainly because of the corruption of the Lincoln County sheriff, who was in the pocket of Dolan and Murphy.

What Jesse did not realize was that his killing of Tunstall opened the gates and let hell enter Lincoln County. The murder of Tunstall was just the opening salvo in the violence that became the Lincoln County War.

The Lincoln County War was not truly a cattle war or a land war, although in some ways it was a war for both. Ultimately, it was a war for economic supremacy. Until John Tunstall and his partner Alexander McSween showed up, J. J. Dolan and Lawrence Murphy had owned the only mercantile store in the Lincoln County area, a huge land section in eastern New Mexico Territory. In addition, they held false claims to thousands of acres of land and sold them illegally to unsuspecting settlers.

Dolan and Murphy had control over the government's Indian contracts, the local farmers' crops, and settlers in Lincoln County. And during the 1800s Lincoln County was the largest in the New Mexico Territory, covering about one-quarter of the region. That was a sizeable chunk of land to control.

Not only did Murphy and Dolan have a monopoly on goods and contracts, they also controlled the local law enforcement and had strong ties to the Santa Fe Ring.

For years the federal government had complained about the poor quality of goods that Murphy and Dolan delivered on their Indian contracts. They also believed the outfit was charging them exorbitant prices. It was not until Tunstall came to town and established his ranch and mercantile store that the government and the locals had a choice. Another element colored the relationship between Dolan and Murphy, Tunstall and McSween. The Irishmen emigrated from their home country and were of working-class stock. Tunstall came from a posh English family, and McSween was a lawyer with Scottish parents.

At the time ethnic bigotry was unlabeled but overt. In a letter to his parents, John Tunstall described Sheriff Brady as "an Irishman, a slave of whiskey and a man I think very little of, he is a tool." He used Brady's ethnicity as a slight.

The animosity between the owners of the two stores started soon after Tunstall's arrival. It did not take long before both sides armed themselves with men who had guns and knew how to use them. And there were a number of rough men around the territory with suspect pasts, men who were willing to lend their guns for a cause, if the price was right. In this case the price was right for Evans and his boys.

The coroner's inquest on Tunstall's murder concluded that Jesse Evans, Frank Baker, Thomas Hill, George Hindman, James J. Dolan, and William Morton shot Tunstall. Eyewitnesses identified them all as being involved in the murder. These outlaws were all members of "The House," a name given to the supporters of Murphy and Dolan. Members of the opposite faction who supported Tunstall and McSween were called "The Regulators."

When the constable, Atanacio Martinez, went to arrest Tunstall's murderers, Sheriff Brady refused to let him serve the warrants and in fact arrested Billy the Kid and Fred Waite, who accompanied the constable. When they asked Brady why he arrested the men, he replied, "Because I had the power." During the next five months, threats, shootings, illegal arrests, and confrontations boiled tempers in Lincoln. In early March, Dick Brewer and a posse of McSween sympathizers arrested Morton and Baker at the Dolan cow camp near the Pecos River. Unfortunately, the two never stood trial; they were shot, killed, and buried on the trail to Lincoln. Some say they tried to escape; others say that the Dolan faction had them killed so they "wouldn't talk."

Meanwhile, Evans and his pal Tom Hill were going on about their business—the business of robbing, rustling, and stealing, that is. They raided a sheep camp belonging to John Wagner, a German immigrant. While they were busy looting, the shepherd unexpectedly returned. Grabbing a rifle Hill had left leaning against a tree, Wagner shot and killed Tom Hill and wounded Evans.

Evans escaped but decided to turn himself in at Fort Stanton, where he could get the medical attention he needed. If accused of the Tunstall murder, he planned to blame the now-dead Tom Hill. The military jailed Evans when he showed up at Fort Stanton; however, it wasn't long before Evans bribed a guard and was once again free.

On April 1 the two factions moved closer to war when Billy the Kid and other Tunstall loyalists ambushed and killed Sheriff Brady and George Hindman. The list of men responsible for the murder of Tunstall was getting shorter.

After Brady's death George Pippin became sheriff. He immediately made it clear that he was a Dolan–Murphy man by arresting McSween on a trumped-up charge of assault. The charge was ridiculous, and McSween was quickly released.

In mid-April of 1878, a grand jury of the Supreme Court of the territory finally indicted Jesse Evans, George Davis, Miguel Seguero, and Frank Rivers for the murder of John Tunstall. Evans was the only one of the group who could be located. He was arrested, and a bond was set at $5,000—an easy sum for Evans and his powerful friends to raise. Once again, Evans was a free man.

The federal government in Washington was aware that things were spinning out of control in the territory and sent Judge Frank Warner Angel, a special investigator, to look into the Tunstall murder and the operations of the Dolan and Murphy group. Angel reported that "there is no doubt that Wm. Morton, Jesse Evans and Tom Hill were the only persons present and saw the shooting, and that two of these persons murdered him . . . " Since Morton and Hill were dead, that left only Evans to face the charges.

Things in Lincoln County came to a head on July 14, 1878. The Regulators set up several fortified places and sealed off the east end of town. Sheriff Pippin sent for his men, who were out of town trying to locate McSween and his cronies. They came in the west end of town and set up their defenses.

The battle lasted for five days. The first four days saw few casualties: a dead man from The House, a dead horse, a dead mule, and the accidental wounding of a young man who got in the way of the fight. It was on the evening of July 19 that Pippin's group made its move: They set the McSween stronghold on fire.

McSween waited until early morning, and as flames engulfed the building, he attempted to escape into the darkness. As he darted out the front door, he met a barrage of bullets and was killed instantly.

By the end of the fighting, men from both sides of the war were dead: McSween, Morton, Baker, McCloskey, Hill, Sheriff Brady, Hindman, Roberts, Brewer, and John Middleton. Billy the Kid and Jesse Evans, who fought on opposite sides of the battle, sustained only minor wounds. And with both Tunstall and McSween now dead, the Lincoln County War ended.

The next morning some of Dolan's men broke into the Tunstall store. When the store clerk showed up, he found Evans in his underwear trying on a new suit of clothes he had picked off the rack.

In December 1878 Billy the Kid decided to return to Lincoln and make peace with Jesse Evans. He set up a meeting with Dolan and Evans. After dark Evans met Billy the Kid in the middle of the street. "I ought to kill you right now," Evans told Billy. The Kid did not scare easily, though, and he recognized the statement for bluster on Jesse's part.

Jesse and Billy agreed to end their fighting and to not testify against the other. There was quite a group of tough men in town that night. Both men brought friends with them for support. After Billy and Evans agreed to a truce, the group decided to celebrate. Billy, a nondrinker, was soon the only sober one.

Evans had a new member of his gang, a young, foolish kid by the name of Billy Campbell. Campbell was not around for the Lincoln County War and deeply regretted the lost opportunity to prove his manhood.

In the middle of the celebration, Huston Chapman walked out of his house. Chapman was an abrasive, aggressive man. Campbell put his pistol on Chapman's chest and said "dance." Chapman was not going to let this rabble bully him. There was some scuffling and some insults and then Dolan, standing behind Chapman, fired at the same time as Campbell. Chapman staggered and fell to the ground.

There are two versions of what happened next. Some report that the two gunmen fired so closely together that they set off a powder keg near Chapman. Others report that someone poured whiskey on Chapman's body and set fire to it. The results were the same: Chapman was burnt to a cinder.

The Chapman murder is what finally convinced the territorial governor to do something about the lawlessness in Lincoln. He instructed the commander of Fort Stanton to round up thirty-five desperados. Included on the list were Billy the Kid, Tom O'Folliard, Dolan, Campbell, and Evans. Billy the Kid and O'Folliard managed to give the authorities the slip. Dolan, Campbell, and Evans were not so lucky. Authorities arrested them and hauled them into jail.

Billy the Kid, now completely disgusted with Evans and not trusting him, worked a deal with the governor, giving testimony against Evans for the promise of amnesty. His testimony helped indict the trio. However, the three did not spend much time as the guests of the county. They escaped from the Fort Stanton jail during the night of March 19, 1879, and a freed Evans lit out for Pecos County, Texas.

For four months Evans kept to his ways: stealing cattle, robbing stores, and following a lawless and unrepentant life. On July 3, 1880, the Texas Rangers got information on Evans's hideout. The pursuit of Evans resulted in the death of two Rangers; one of them, Red Bingham, was shot by Evans; the other by an unidentified outlaw Evans was riding with.

It took the Rangers nine days, but they finally captured Evans and locked him in the "bat cave," a dungeon blasted out of rock in the jail. Evans would never break out of this cell; the cave was beneath the sheriff's office, and a trapdoor covered with heavy timbers was the only way in and out.

On October 9, 1880, the state of Texas sentenced Evans to ten years in the state prison in Huntsville, Texas, for the murder of Red Bingham. But just two years later, Evans worked his magic one final time. He escaped from a road gang in May 1882 and disappeared.

But Jesse Evans was too bad a man and too colorful an outlaw to be forgotten. Over the years, rumors popped up about him. Some say he was seen in Tombstone, Arizona Territory, in 1882 or 1883. Others believed he went to live on a relative's ranch and left the house only at night. The best rumor involved a man named Bushy Bill Roberts and concerned the strong physical resemblance between Billy the Kid and Evans. Both were small in statue, standing less than five foot seven and weighing around 150 pounds. Both had fair hair and light complexions. However, their personalities were quite different. Evans was surly, unfriendly, and almost illiterate. Billy the Kid was an avid reader, wrote a fine hand, loved to sing, and was friendly and outgoing.

Bushy Bill claimed to be Billy the Kid. While Bushy knew much about Billy, there were many factual holes in his claim. However, the only Anglo in the Lincoln County War not accounted for was Evans. And Bushy Bill knew too many details about the war to have just read about it. He had to have been in Lincoln at the time. That leads some to think that Bushy Bill was really Jesse Evans. Now wouldn't that be something—Jesse Evans making the ultimate escape, removing his identity by impersonating his old friend and enemy Billy the Kid?

"Mysterious" Dave Mather

Lawman or Gunman?

Dave Mather was an enigma. Some called him friend, but he confided in and trusted no one. At times he was a lawman; at other times an outlaw; sometimes he was suspected of being both at the same time. He was an opportunist acting on whatever side of the law was the most profitable. Mather would disappear after a robbery or cattle rustling had taken place and then reappear later. It got folks to wondering where he had been and what he had been up to. His elusive behavior earned him the moniker "Mysterious" Dave Mather.

Mather was born in Connecticut in either 1845 or 1851 and was the oldest of three boys; the youngest died when he was a year old. Mather's father was a seaman who died in 1864, having abandoned his family eight years earlier. Sometime in the late 1850s his mother took another husband. When she died in 1868, the two remaining brothers ran away to sea but jumped ship after less than a year of sailor life. That's when Dave started his western wanderings.

He worked and traveled through Arkansas, Texas, Kansas, Colorado, and New Mexico. He was his own man, taking whatever path or action he chose without regard to morals, laws, or the demands of others. This silent man had few friends but many acquaintances, including Wyatt Earp, Bat Masterson, "Dirty" Dave Rudabaugh, and Hoodoo Brown. Yet no one really knew him well.

In the 1870s one of the wildest towns in the West was Las Vegas, New Mexico. Word was that if you were looking for trouble, you were guaranteed to find it there—just like you would find gunfighters, bad men, cardsharps, prostitutes, and just about any other kind of evil.

It was July 1879 when Mather rode into Las Vegas. Townsfolk saw a small man with fragile-looking shoulders, a thin frame, and a short stature. His hair was an ordinary brown. His only distinguishing feature was his long, droopy mustache. But those who looked in his eyes were more cautious. He had the hard, determined look of a dangerous gunslinger.

Mather joined the Dodge City Gang, led by Hoodoo Brown. The gang had originally been the law in Dodge City until its citizens got tired of crime, corruption, and favoritism. They ran Brown and his cohorts out of town, and the gang settled in Las Vegas, a town friendlier to their type of law.

Las Vegas citizens first heard about Mather on August 14, 1879, when he was charged with aiding in a nearby train robbery. When the prosecution failed to appear, he was released. Immediately afterward he secured an appointment as a lawman, a Las Vegas deputy for town Marshal Joe Carson.

Sometime in November, Mather arrested a group of drunken soldiers for disorderly conduct. One soldier tried to escape. Running down the street, he repeatedly fired his gun. Mather, who was a crack shot, slowed the soldier down by sending a spray of bullets down the street at him, one of which hit the soldier's thumb. The wound subdued the soldier, and he was taken to the jail.

The *Las Vegas Gazette* mildly rebuked Mather for the incautious way he sent bullets flying down the town's street and accused him of taking too aggressive an action. Mather defended his action, claiming the soldier shot first, and, just like that, the matter was closed.

Mather's next encounter as a lawman, in January 1881, was far more serious. The Henry Gang, another collection of hoodlums, had come to town. The gang ignored the slight man wearing a deputy badge. He seemed too small, too quiet to matter. This was the wrong move, and they paid for it dearly. Mather was quick on the draw and one of the West's most accurate shooters.

A serious Mysterious Dave
Courtesy of Kansas State Historical Society

The Henry Gang included Thomas Jefferson House (aka Tom Henry), John Dorsey, James Lowe (aka James West), and William "Big" Randall. They had been in town for several days and were blind with booze when they walked into the Close and Patterson Saloon late in the evening of January 22.

Despite being previously warned by Marshal Joe Carson about wearing their shooting irons in public, the gang stumbled into the saloon with their guns in plain sight. Alerted to the crime, Carson and Deputy Mather entered the saloon, approached the Henry Gang boys, and told them they were breaking a town ordinance. The gang was told that the guns had to be deposited behind the bar and that they could claim them on their way out.

Those instructions did not please the Henry Gang, and lead started flying. The first to be hit was Joe Carson; a bullet broke his arm. He put his gun in his left hand, but a second shot broke his left arm. He stood there defenseless as the gang pumped eight bullets into his body. Without a word he walked to the door and fell down dead.

Meanwhile, someone took a shot at Mather, which went harmlessly through his coat. He returned the fire and killed William Randall, shot Jim West in his right lung and liver, and put two bullets in Tom Henry's leg. Despite his wounds Tom Henry and his partner John Dorsey escaped, making their way to the Lewelling and Olds corral. Once there, they saddled up and hightailed it out of town.

During the fight the lights were shot out. When they were relit, a scene of carnage greeted the viewers: Joe Carson's body blocked the doorway; Randall's body laid near the stove, his guns unfired; and Jim West lay dying.

If West thought he would get some compassion from Mather for his wounded state, he was sadly mistaken. Mather ordered West to be taken directly to jail rather than to the hospital. Once in jail, Mather sent for the doctor, who determined that West had no hope for survival. West lay in jail slowly dying.

Three days after the saloon fight, a crew of railroad graders came to town with the railroad telegraph operator, Joe Castello. Ordinarily Joe was pretty sensible and strove to keep his fellow workers out of trouble. But several days of drinking had dulled his senses.

Two of Joe's men got into a fistfight. In his attempt to separate them, Joe drew his revolver and waved it at the crowd that was gathering. Mather ordered everyone to holster their guns. Castello, who was well lit from liquor, pointed his cocked pistol at Mysterious Dave. Mather immediately fired, and the ball passed through Castello's left side—through his lung, stomach, and liver. Castello died the following morning. The coroner's jury found that "the deceased came to his death by a pistol shot fired from a pistol in the hands of D. H. Mather, constable, in the discharge of his duty as an officer; and that said shooting was justifiable and in self protection."

Mather was viewed as a hero by the town for standing up to the Henry Gang, killing one man and seriously wounding another in a darkened saloon gunfight. He had faced down a cocked pistol pointed at his heart, and in one shot ended what the town thought could have been a serious gunfight with the railroad men.

On February 22 Mather received a tip that the killers of Carson were hiding in Mora. He mounted a posse with J. J. Webb, Dutchy Goodlet, Dave Rudabaugh, Lee Smith, Harry Coombs, and a man named Muldoon.

The posse surrounded the gunmen's hideout and after much discussion, Henry and Dorsey surrendered with the assurance that they would receive guaranteed protection from vigilante action. They were willing to take their chances with the legal system. The two men were sent to jail, where they joined fellow gang member West, who was still in the process of dying.

The *Las Vegas Optic* printed a few words on the capture of the men, pronouncing that they would be "jerked to Jesus before the sun rises again."

At about 2:30 A.M. the day after the men's imprisonment, a masked lynch mob took the prisoners from the jail. It was reported but never proven that Mather was the leader. The prisoners were immediately hanged from a windmill that stood in the plaza. The next day the jury report confirmed that the men were taken from jail and killed by an unknown mob

Mather's next action as a deputy came in response to an argument over breakfast. Mather was helping the St. Nicholas Hotel set up tables when the waiter, an ill-tempered young man of twenty, got into an argument with a liquor salesman by the name of James Moorhead.

Moorhead ordered eggs. Johnny Alan, the waiter, said it was too late for the cook to prepare them. The argument escalated into a pushing and shoving match. They parted and Moorhead headed for the office to complain, while Alan went into the dining room to get his pistol.

When Moorhead came out of the office, Alan pointed the gun at Moorhead and told him to get down on his knees and apologize. Again they struggled, and Alan's gun went off, fatally wounding Moorhead. Having witnessed the entire incident, Mather arrested Alan. The *Las Vegas Gazette* reported that "Alan was arrested by an officer, being found in the dining-room, quietly preparing the table for dinner." Neither man had noticed the slight man working.

Meanwhile, the excitement in town over the breakfast murder gave J. J. Webb and Dutchy Goodlet the cover they needed to plan and execute the robbery of newcomer Michael Keliher, a man known to carry a great deal of money. They enlisted the help of a man called Boyle. Boyle invited Keliher to drink with him at the Goodlet and Robinson Saloon. After a few drinks Boyle picked a fight with Keliher, and Webb and Goodlet rushed in and shot Keliher for "disturbing the peace." It just so happened that when Webb caught the falling Keliher, his wallet fell into Webb's hands. Mather was required to arrest both of his lawmen pals for murder.

Arresting pals was more than a man like Mather could take.

Immediately after the arrest, he resigned his position and took the train out of town. He left for the gold fields of Colorado Territory.

Mather wandered through various towns in Kansas, returning to the good side of the law as the city marshal in New Kiowa, Kansas, and then spent the next few years involved in various nefarious schemes. He spent time gambling in Colorado, was accused of counterfeiting in Texas, and dabbled in law enforcement in El Paso. From El Paso he headed for Dallas, where he spent his leisure time with Georgia Morgan. Morgan was the black proprietress of the Long Branch, a famous sporting house. Mather did some pimping, or "blacksmithing," as it was called, for her, but the relationship abruptly ended when he tried to leave town with Morgan's gold ring and chain.

Morgan wasn't going to let him off easily. She followed him and caused such a public disturbance when she found him that she was fined $8.25. Mather seized the opportunity to make his escape but was pulled off the train by the law and returned to Dallas. Morgan decided enough was enough and never brought charges. Again Mather was a free man. After the incident with Morgan, Mather headed to Dodge City and took over another lawman position as assistant marshal. He also became co-owner of the Opera House Saloon on Front Street.

A town ordinance was passed that favored his competitor and enemy, saloon owner Tom Nixon. Nixon resented Mather's business and also accused Mather of paying too much attention to his wife. The two men had an unfriendly encounter outside the Opera House Saloon. Nixon drew his gun and fired at Mather, who was wounded by the powder burns and a flying splinter. Nixon fled, gleefully bragging that he had killed Mather.

Nixon was found, arrested, and charged with "assault to kill." He was released on bail to wait the next term of court. Acquaintances warned Nixon to watch out. He was told that Mather was a dangerous man to have for an enemy. With bravado Nixon taunted Mather by walking past the Opera House Saloon. Mather spotted him, walked out of the saloon, said, "Hello, Tom," and put three shots into him. Bill Tilghman, the town marshal, ran up before the echo of the shots had died down. Mather willingly turned his guns over with the comment that he "ought to have killed him six months ago." A hearing bound Mather over for trial. He was released on $6,000 bail. The case came to trial in January 1885, and Mather was found not guilty. But that was not the end of Mather's run-ins with the law in Dodge.

It was at the Junction Saloon that a few games of chance went wrong. A disagreement between Mather's brother, Cy, and a man named Dave Barnes led to a shootout that left Barnes dead. Both brothers were arrested, although Dave Mather had never fired a shot.

While Mather was stewing in jail, the men in Dodge began enhancing his life with interesting creative tales. New arrivals in town would soon hear about how bad Mather was, and then the details of the Barnes–Mather fight would be spun out. In the town version a stray bullet in the fight had killed a famous greyhound. When his owner, James Kelley, was told about the demise of his dog, he was furious and swore to hunt Mather down for the murder of the defenseless animal. The story went that the town held an official inquest and buried the dog with full honors. The assigned coroner, O. B. Joyful Brown, impaneled a jury to settle the matter. A witness testified that the dog had never been known to drink. Another said if that were true, than what was he doing in a saloon? A third man testified that Mather's gun had misfired and that the dog could have jumped out of harm's way. The jury reached the decision that the dog "came to its death by a bullet fired from a gun in the hands of Dave Mather, better known as Mysterious Dave, and that the shooting was justified as any dog should know better than to go to sleep in a Dodge City saloon." It is not known what Mather thought of this tall tale.

This was not the first time the reprobates of Dodge picked on Mather. He was a solitary man with quirky habits, and he made an easy target. He liked to sit by himself in the local saloons; across the street from one of them hung the town fire bell. Mather would periodically test his aim by taking out his gun and shooting at the bell. When he could no longer make it ring, he figured he was drunk and would head for home. One night the bartender loaded Dave's weapon with blanks. When Dave tried to ring the bell, nothing happened. He got on his horse and headed for home. Spotting a coyote on the trail he aimed, fired, and of course, nothing happened. It was a good while before Dave took another drink.

One particular incident had the townspeople grinning for days. It was Mather's religious "salvation." A preacher by the name of Johnson was in town on a mission to convert the wickedest man there. The townsmen decided that Mather had earned the honor. Never an hour went by that one of them didn't remind Mather that he needed saving. Bat Masterson confronted him in the local saloon and with some fast-talking, aided by the other gamblers, finally convinced Mather to seek redemption.

That night, Mather went to church at the Lady Gay Dancehall. After all the preaching and hymn singing was done, Preacher Johnson asked the congregation who would bear witness to his faith.

Mather was sitting in a prominent front-row seat, and as if on cue, he rose up and announced that he had seen the error of his ways and was now converted. The preacher was delighted and announced that had Mather remained the way he was, he should have been afraid to die. "You mean I don't need to be afraid now?" Mather asked the preacher. "Oh no," he was assured. Hearing that happy announcement, Mather drew his gun, pointed it at the preacher, and asked him if he was afraid to go with him.

When Mather shot out the lanterns, the preacher jumped through the window, and Mather left muttering about a "bunch of hypocrites." The town's gamblers and gunmen thought this was a good joke on the preacher, and they made sure the story circulated.

Back in the town jail Mather and his brother awaited bail for the Barnes killing. Bail had been set at $3,000 each, and the trial was scheduled for

December. After he was freed on bail, Mather walked out of the Dodge City jail on a cold winter day and was never seen again, although there were rumors about him. From time to time, sightings of Mather were reported. James Kerr, a hardware clerk in Long Pine, Nebraska, insisted he let Dave live in his wilderness cabin. It was reported that when Mather needed money, he would work at the railroad depot hotel in town, but other than that, he led a solitary life in the woods. Another story reported that Mather had joined the North West Canadian Mounted Police. The most interesting speculation is that Mather was abducted by an unidentified flying object. The man who many considered a mystery managed to remain one for the rest of his life.

The Stockton Brothers
The Death of a Party

The Stockton brothers' favorite activity was cattle rustling. However, murder seemed to run a close second. The boys roamed from Texas to the Colorado and New Mexico Territories, and in every western town they stopped, they found trouble.

Outlaw behavior was not something the Stocktons came to as adults. Even as children the brothers were drawn to the wrong side of the law. Separately and together, early and late, they made trouble of the worse kind.

Ike and Porter started their lives as the sons of a Texas rancher, a life they had no liking for. Porter Stockton, the youngest, was born in Erath County, Texas, in 1854. Both boys spent their early years near Cleburne, Texas. As children the two of them were wild and hard to control. As young men they were independent, uncontrollable, and greedy. Their quick tempers led them to take chances and produced results that were dangerous.

Rumor had it that Porter killed his first man when he was twelve. When he was seventeen, the law caught up with him, and he was charged with attempted murder. He was sent to jail on that charge, but the case never came to trial. Ike helped him escape, and the two headed for Dodge City, a breeding ground for the worst outlaws in the land. Ike was a responsible older brother. He looked after Porter by including him in his ventures and rescuing him from jail whenever he got into trouble with the law.

When they tired of Dodge, the brothers headed for Lincoln County in New Mexico Territory, where they opened a saloon. It was a turbulent time, and the region was torn by two factions—the Dolan gang and the McSween group—who were fighting over government contracts. It

31

was a conflict that erupted into a war that lasted more than five months and included such famous participants as Billy the Kid, Pat Garrett, Jose Chavez, Dave Rudabaugh, and George and Frank Coe. If you wanted to meet the lawless, Lincoln County was the place to be at that time. Most of the prime outlaws of the land either passed through Lincoln or stayed and picked a side. The Stocktons didn't actually pick a side, but they were in the middle of the action.

With all of the criminal activity going on, Ike and Porter eventually decided to leave Lincoln County. They sold their saloon and headed for Trinidad, Colorado Territory. By this time Ike was a married man with a family. Porter figured it was time he followed suit. He picked out the daughter of a Baptist preacher, Irma, and the two married.

Next, Porter wandered over to Cimarron. It was October 1876, and he found trouble again. In the town's Lambert's Saloon, he lit the fuse of his ever-simmering temper. He and a man by the name of Juan Gonzales got into an explosive argument. Porter brought his guns out firing, killing Gonzales on the spot. When the body was examined, it was found that Gonzales was unarmed. Porter beat a hasty retreat out of town.

Two months later, in December, Porter was back in Trinidad and took to his guns again. This time it was in the barroom of the St. James Hotel. An afternoon of card playing and drinking had ended in an argument with another player. The other man was not armed, but that didn't even slow down the enraged Porter. He whipped out his gun and shot the other man in cold blood and hot fury.

Porter escaped the saloon but was soon captured by a posse that brought him in and slapped him in jail. Brother Ike came to the rescue again and broke him out. Now Trinidad was no longer a hospitable town for the Stockton brothers. It was time for another move.

Next stop was the Durango area of the Colorado Territory. Durango was a supply town for the large ranches nearby. It was fairly safe and quiet during the week, but when the weekend came, the town took on a different personality. It was full of dust and six-guns as miners and cowboys

The Montano Store in Lincoln, New Mexico, where the Stocktons owned a saloon
Carl Sheppard Photo, Courtesy Palace of the Governors (MNM/DCA), #122909

came to town looking for a good time and ways to spend their money. Rough men seeking ways to have fun—and not giving a damn how always spelled trouble.

The Durango gangs and the Farmington gunslingers were continually having shootouts, presenting a constant danger to the innocent and honest citizens of Durango. Ike Stockton's gang fit right in.

The Stockton gang operated in an area that covered Durango, Colorado Territory, and Farmington, New Mexico Territory. The gang was involved in a number of crimes, including cattle rustling, train robbing, and murder. They would commit a crime in Colorado then hightail it across the territory line to escape pursuit, reversing the process when necessary.

Finally, the Durango townspeople mounted a campaign, led by the female editor of the local paper, to get the rough element out of town.

This pressure forced the Stockton gang to leave Durango and move into Silverton. That town soon withdrew its hospitality when the Stocktons killed the town sheriff. A reward was immediately posted for their capture: A price of $2,500 was placed on the head of each gang member.

When they left Silverton, Porter and Ike split. Porter went to Animas City, where he managed to get appointed town marshal. Animas City was originally picked to be a railroad hub in the region, but its townspeople objected to the railroad's demands for free land and donations. So the railroad purchased land nearby and built its own town, calling it Durango.

Porter lost his marshal job when the residents ran him out of town for chasing the town barber down the street, shooting to kill. Porter had worked up a good temper when the barber accidentally nicked him during a shave.

Porter's next stop was Rico, Colorado Territory. Here he briefly held the job of town marshal. It didn't take long for word to reach Rico of Porter's past, and the townsfolk didn't feel too safe with an outlaw for marshal. They fired him and ran him out of town. After that incident it was apparent to Porter that Colorado was not a friendly place for him to be. That's when he, his wife Irma, and their two baby daughters moved near to Farmington in the New Mexico Territory. Ike, his family, and his outlaw friends settled near Durango.

All this lawless activity in the area of the Colorado and New Mexico border had gotten the attention of New Mexico's governor, who was tired of the Stockton gang. Governor Wallace formed a local militia group called the San Juan Guard. Their job was to patrol the roads between the territories of New Mexico and Colorado. One of their primary missions was the capture of the Stockton gang.

The big ranchers had also had enough of disappearing stock. They decided to take matters into their own hands. They formed the Stockman's Association and backed their group with guns; these were the guns that eventually killed Porter Stockton at his Farmington ranch.

What brought down Porter started out as a Christmas celebration. Frank Hamblet, Stockton's neighbor, started thinking about the coming holidays. He figured they would be a good time to gather friends and neighbors before the dreariness of the wet, cold winter set in. He decided that the party invitations should be distributed to neighbors in the next few days. That brought his thoughts around to the one neighbor he wanted nothing to do with, Porter Stockton.

Hamblet knew Porter was a nasty man known for his uncontrollable and undisciplined behavior—definitely not the sort you would want at a happy, festive celebration. Besides, Hamblet didn't care for the way Porter had acquired his ranch. Porter, his wife, and their two children had recently taken over a rundown ranch outside Farmington. Propped up on the land was a decrepit shack. When the widow, who owned the land, left to visit relatives, Porter simply moved into her shack and claimed her land. Then, with the help of his pals, he stocked his ranch with some cattle belonging to Frank Simmons, another Farmington rancher. Of course this was done without Simmons's permission.

Simmons reclaimed the cattle, but bad blood remained between Stockton and Simmons. The two sides—the Simmons gang and the Stockton gang—decided to settle their differences in a gun battle on the streets of Durango. The shootout was fast and furious, and outlaw-wary citizens took refuge. A baker hid his children in an oven to protect them; bankers locked up their assets in vaults; all citizens cleared the streets. The battle ended abruptly when both sides ran out of ammunition. There were some minor wounds but nothing serious, and both gangs rode out of town into the sunset.

Now, months later, Porter was welcoming a couple of old pals who had come to visit his ranch and do some business. The "business" they had in mind was cattle—someone else's cattle. The visitors, Harge Eskridge, James Garret, and Oscar Pruitt, were all members of Ike Stockton's gang.

Porter was pleased to see them, and he decided to show them a good time for the holidays. He figured a party was the best form of entertainment and decided to crash the Hamblets'. It didn't matter to Porter that Hamblet had never sent him an invitation. That detail wasn't going to stop him and his friends from joining in the fun. Unfortunately, the forgotten invitation to Porter was not an oversight on Frank Hamblet's part; it was a deliberate snub.

The night of the party, Porter and his less savory friends mounted up and headed for the Hamblet ranch. Music from the party floated on the night air, drawing the riders in. The festivities were in full swing when the four men rode into the Hamblets' front yard. They swung down from their horses and swaggered into the cabin for the party. Porter and his cowboy companions were fully armed. The other men at Hamblet's had no weapons; they had come to party, not to fight.

Porter and friends entered the Hamblets' house and quickly became as obnoxious as possible. They pulled sweethearts, wives, mothers, and sisters into their arms for dancing. The women were appalled and frightened, the menfolk angry. Hamblet's temper was about to boil over. He reminded Porter that he and his friends had not been invited and demanded that they leave immediately.

Eventually, the four party crashers made their way back outside, where the party was continuing. First thing they did was pull out their six-shooters and start popping shots off into the crowd of dancers. A stray shot hit Porter's friend Pruitt, who died on the spot. Another killed one of the guests, George Brown, the son of Doctor John W. Brown of Farmington.

By this time it was apparent—even to Stockton and his pals—that things had gotten out of hand. The three remaining intruders hastily rode away, leaving two dead men and a shattered holiday party behind.

Ranchers in the neighborhood were shocked by Stockton's actions. Victim George Brown was a respected young man, well liked by all who knew him—and his friends wanted his death avenged. A $1,000 reward was raised for the capture of Stockton, Eskridge, and Garret.

On January 4, 1881, County Sheriff Alf Graves, accompanied by eighteen men who were all connected to the Stockman's Association, rode to Porter Stockton's ranch. Some say these men were out looking for cattle rustlers, and the trail took them right to Stockton's. Others say that Graves and Porter had had an argument, and Graves rode to the ranch to seek Porter out and settle the dispute. There was also talk that the posse was looking to avenge the Christmas party murders.

When the posse arrived at Porter's ranch house, Sheriff Graves shouted for him to come out. In answer Stockton stepped out of his cabin, rifle in hand, pumping lead. The posse returned fire, and Porter dropped to the ground dead within view of his wife, his body riddled with bullets.

In hysterics Porter's wife rushed out of the cabin, picked up her husband's rifle, and taking refuge behind a wagon, began firing. The few shots she got off went wild. Sheriff Graves peeled off another shot, and this one hit a wagon spoke near Irma, spraying splinters into her face and arm. They stung her shooting hand, and she dropped her rifle. That ended the shootout. The injury Irma Stockton received rendered her arm useless and crippled her for life. Years later she died from complications caused by the wound.

When Ike Stockton heard about the death of his brother, he vowed revenge on the posse that killed him. He gathered a group of gunslingers and went hunting. He so terrorized the citizens around Farmington that armed patrols were set up to guard the streets.

During this time cattle began disappearing from local ranches, folks were shot at for no reason, and Ike and his gang were being blamed for it all. In a move to eliminate the lawlessness in his territory, Governor Lew Wallace offered a reward for the arrest of the Stockton gang.

The gang was able to elude authorities for a time. Ike and his band continued their activities around Farmington and Durango, killing several of the posse members. But their success made them overconfident.

In September, nine months after his brother's death, Ike rode into

Durango for supplies. He wasn't as anonymous as he liked to think. Someone recognized him and reported to the sheriff that the notorious Ike Stockton was in town.

The gun battle that followed in the streets of Durango won Ike a bullet that shattered his left knee. The town doctor amputated the leg, hoping to save Ike's life, but Ike never made it—he died within a few hours of the injury.

What was left of Ike's gang moved on to Socorro, but much to their dismay, their fame had spread. They were quickly recognized and strung up by the town's vigilante group. The Stockton brothers' lives ended within months of each other. It seems fate worked to keep them together. They lived and worked together in lawlessness, and they both met their maker at the hands of the law.

Vengeance brought down Ike, but for Porter it was a Christmas party that led him to his final resting place, six feet under New Mexico land.

"Dirty" Dave Rudabaugh
The Dirtiest Outlaw of All

Dave Rudabaugh didn't have much use for water. He didn't use it to wash, brush his teeth, or clean his clothes, and he sure as hell was not going to drink it. Give him the pure fire of whiskey anytime. Dirty Dave came by his nickname honestly.

Maybe that explains why he was such a drifter—he was a hard man to be around for any length of time. People always knew when Dirty Dave was coming; his scent preceded him.

However, not everyone saw Dave as an unkempt character. In 1882, a *Denver Tribune* reporter described him in these flattering terms:

He is thick set and athletic in build; is about five-feet nine-inches in height. He is suave and very gentlemanly in his deportment. He has brown hair, hazel eyes and a heavy mustache of a shade of brown lighter than that of his hair.

He is fluent in speech, mildly argumentative in disposition, and has that peculiar faculty of being able to obtain news and facts where others would fail. This is a faculty which he uses advantageously in his search for express news on railroads.

He is as brave as a lion and a natural born organizer. He gathers a gang and has it in working condition within a few days. He is always clear-headed, has the cunning of a fox, and never falls into a position of unnecessary danger through the recklessness of bravery or dissipation.

Considering Dirty Dave's criminal activities, this article was obviously the writing of a very creative reporter. About the only thing he got right was the description of Rudabaugh's lush mustache.

Rudabaugh was born in Illinois in 1854. His father was killed in the Civil War, and Rudabaugh grew up poor and uneducated. By the time he was twenty-six, he had a variety of lawless occupations on his resume—cattle rustling in Texas, train robbery in Kansas, and gambling wherever he managed to find a deck of cards and a seat for his unwashed body. To balance out the bad, he sometimes worked with the law instead of against it. However, most of his law enforcement activities were with sheriffs whose honesty was questionable.

Rudabaugh wasn't big on loyalty. On several occasions he turned against his partners, giving evidence to the law to save his own skin. They say that these unprincipled characteristics paired with his accuracy with a gun earned him the fear of the notorious Billy the Kid.

Dirty Dave was not a big planner or thinker. It was this unpredictability that set off a series of events that proved to be his downfall.

When the citizens of Dodge City, Kansas, decided to clean up their town, Las Vegas in the New Mexico Territory became the destination for many of Dodge's unsavory characters. In 1880 Las Vegas was as wild as any western town could be, and the Dodge City gang members took control. They terrorized the residents and elected themselves as town officials. The gang consisted of Justice of the Peace H. G. Neill, also known as Hoodoo Brown; Marshall Dutchy Goodlet; and Constable Dave Mather. Dirty Dave, Tom Pickett, and J. J. Webb were hired on as special officers. These "lawmen" were frequently involved in murder, train robberies, and cattle rustling.

Easy money was always a lure for the Dodge City boys, and one day Webb, with the help of Dutchy Goodlet, decided to relieve Michael Keliher, a visiting traveling salesman, of the large amount of cash he was carrying. They enlisted the aid of a railroad worker named Boyle. The plan was for Boyle to pick a fight with Keliher while the two were

drinking; Webb and Goodlet would rush in, arrest Keliher for disturbing the peace, and relieve him of his cash. The plan went terribly wrong;
in their excitement to get the job done, Webb and Goodlet barged into
the saloon and killed Keliher.

Much to the surprise of Webb and Goodlet, their pals Dave Mather
and Dave Rudabaugh arrested them for murder. Mather was so disgusted with the outcome of these events that he quit the police force and
left town. Rudabaugh decided to take a more hands-on approach by
freeing J. J. Webb from jail. Just because the "law" required him to put
his pals in jail didn't mean he believed they should stay there—and with
that in mind, he decided to spring them.

It was in the early morning hours of April 30, 1880, when
Rudabaugh and John "Little Allen" Llewellyn hired a carriage and told
the driver to wait in front of the jail. It was a typical carriage with slow
horses in the traces. Why Rudabaugh picked this means of transporta-
tion considering what he planned to do is a puzzle.

Rudabaugh and Llewellyn entered the jail and asked to see Webb.
The jailer, Antonio Lino-Valdez, allowed Rudabaugh to pass a newspaper to Webb, but when the men told him to hand over the cell key, he
refused. Llewellyn shot and killed him. Tossing the keys in Webb's cell,
both Rudabaugh and Llewellyn made a run for it.

J. J. Webb did some quick thinking. If he ran, the law would hunt
him down; if he stayed, his pending appeal to the Supreme Court might
make him a free man. He decided his best strategy was to stay put.

The two gunmen jumped into the waiting hack and ordered the
driver to take them to East Las Vegas. There they kicked the driver out,
and Rudabaugh took the reins. The first thing they did was to stop at
Houghton's Hardware Store and help themselves to a pair of six-guns
and two rifles.

In the meantime a hastily mounted posse of four men gathered to
pursue the outlaws. Unfortunately, the posse ran out of ammunition
and had to head back to town before they caught the culprits. A larger

posse was soon organized, mounted up, and went on the chase. After traveling twenty-five miles, they came to a sheep camp where they found the abandoned carriage and its horses. The outlaws had stolen two fresh and faster horses, leaving their nags and the carriage with a Mexican shepherd. Here the town posse lost the trail of the murderers.

Rudabaugh and Llewellyn were on the run; their attempted rescue of Webb a complete failure. The jailer was dead, his murderers gone, and J. J. Webb still in jail. They rode hard and long on their flight for freedom. Llewellyn was not a well man, and the ride was taking its toll. He complained constantly about his tuberculosis and rheumatism. He begged Rudabaugh to end his suffering. One day out on the open range, Rudabaugh put a bullet in Llewellyn's head and buried him along the road to Alkali Wells.

From there Dirty Dave made his way to Fort Sumner, New Mexico, and joined Billy the Kid's gang. He soon became the Kid's right-hand man.

Back at the jail, J. J. Webb was having second thoughts about his appeal. Suspecting that vigilantes were sizing up his neck, he made a decision to seek freedom. He and five other prisoners picked the jail lock and escaped. Webb headed for a hideout with fellow prisoner and mule thief George Davis.

Meanwhile, the hunt was on for Billy the Kid. Sheriff Pat Garrett heard the Kid was in the Dedrick ranch house at Bosque Grande on the Pecos River. On November 26, Garrett and his posse surrounded the house. The trap didn't catch Billy, but they did get Webb and Davis, who were hiding in the house. Both were hauled back to the San Miguel jail.

Garrett continued his hunt for the Kid's gang, which now included Rudabaugh along with Billy Wilson, Tom Pickett, Tom O'Folliard, and Charlie Bowdre. Garrett and Frank Stewart, from the Canadian River Cattlemen's Association, received a tip to check Fort Sumner.

Garrett and his posse were settled in the fort and waiting when the six horsemen came in, slowly riding through the snow. The trap was sprung. Garrett and his men opened fire, hitting O'Folliard, a lead rider.

O'Folliard fell and his horse galloped off. The remaining five outlaws turned and hightailed it out of the fort, disappearing in the snowstorm that had increased in intensity.

During the confrontation Rudabaugh's horse was hit, but he rode it until it dropped dead then double-mounted behind Billy Wilson. Back at the fort the posse laid the wounded O'Folliard on a blanket near the fire and settled down to a game of cards. O'Folliard died thirty minutes later.

Stewart and Garrett decided to hold off on following the outlaws until the storm abated. When the storm blew itself out on December 24, they picked up the trail and followed it to an abandoned sheep camp called Stinking Springs, where the outlaws were hanging out.

The camp got its name from a nearby sulfa spring that gave off an odor of rotten eggs. After living with Dirty Dave, the gang hardly noticed the smell.

The outlaws had sought shelter in an abandoned rock house without a door. Billy the Kid's horse was in the house; the other three tied up outside.

The posse arrived at Stinking Springs, and as dawn broke, a man fitting the Kid's description stepped into the doorway. Garrett gave the signal, and the man was riddled with bullets. He staggered, said, "I wish . . . " and then fell dead in the snow. It was then that the posse realized they had shot Charlie Bowdre.

The four inside the shelter settled in to defend themselves, and throughout the morning and early afternoon, the lawmen and the outlaws traded shots.

Garrett noticed that one of the outlaws' horses was slowly moving toward the doorway. When the horse was halfway inside, he fired a quick shot, killing the horse. The horse blocked the doorway, the only entrance in or out of the shelter. The lawmen shot the tethers of the other two horses, who immediately galloped off.

By late afternoon Billy and his remaining gang realized their position was hopeless. They were cold, hungry, and without mounts. A white cloth appeared in the doorway, and after receiving assurances, Dave Rudabaugh came out for a talk. He suggested that the outlaws would surrender if promised food and a safe passage to jail. Garrett and Stewart agreed, and the four prisoners were loaded onto a wagon for the journey to the San Miguel County jail.

On Christmas Day of 1880, the lawmen and what was left of Billy the Kid's gang stopped in Puerto de Luna for a holiday dinner at the home of Roman Catholic priest Alexander Grzelachowski. And on December 26, Billy's gang arrived at the Las Vegas jail.

Both the *Las Vegas Gazette* and *Optic* ran stories on the capture, detailing the excitement of the town as the prisoners rode down the main street. A few days later the *Optic* printed an article describing the four outlaws. Dirty Dave's description read as follows:

> Dave Rudabaugh looks and dresses about the same as when in Las Vegas, apparently not having made any raids upon clothing stores. His face is weather-beaten from long exposure. This is the only noticeable difference. Radubaugh [*sic*] inquired somewhat anxiously in regard to the feeling in the community and was told that it was very strong against him. He remarked that the papers had published exaggerated reports of the depredations of Kid's party in the lower country. It was not half as bad as had been reported.

The prisoners were taken to the railroad station for their train trip to Santa Fe, where they would await trial in the city jail. A large, angry crowd met them at the depot. They wanted Rudabaugh to stand trial in town for the murder of the San Miguel jailer. Las Vegas Sheriff Romero tried to get Rudabaugh off the train and return him to the county jail.

According to a report in the *Optic,* "The engineer of the outgoing train was covered by guns and ordered not to move his engine." However, Rudabaugh was in the hands of a United States Marshall and "they were in duty bound to deliver him to the authorities in Santa Fe."

Rudabaugh went on to Santa Fe where some of his old running mates, including Webb, were awaiting trial for the robbery of two stagecoaches and the attempted robbery of a train, both near Las Vegas.

Rudabaugh went into court to testify in Webb's defense. Rudabaugh admitted that he was the head of the gang that robbed both stages and that Webb was not part of either robbery. His statement won an acquittal for Webb. It also helped free the other men held in connection with the robberies.

Rudabaugh never gave the names of the men who participated in the robberies. Many believed they were the Dodge City boys—"Mysterious" Dave Mather, Joe Carson, and other members of Hoodoo Brown's police force, including Doc Holliday. All this was speculation. There was no proof.

The next day the court indicted Rudabaugh on three charges of robbing the U.S. mail, including two stagecoach robberies and one attempted train robbery. He pleaded guilty to all charges.

On February 26, Rudabaugh's robbery sentence was suspended, and he was ordered returned to the San Miguel County for trial in the death of jailer Antonio Lino-Valdez. An indictment for first-degree murder was waiting for Rudabaugh in Las Vegas.

Rudabaugh had no desire to take his chances in Las Vegas. The time had come for Dirty Dave to seek freedom. Along with Billy the Kid and Billy Wilson, the trio developed a cunning plan.

The Santa Fe *New Mexican* gave a full report in early March 1881:

> Yesterday afternoon it was discovered that the Kid and his gang had concocted and were stealthily carrying out a plan by which they hoped to gain their freedom and escape the fate that awaits them. And very fortunate it was that the discovery was made just when it was, for a night or two more would have sufficed for completion of the well laid scheme. It appears that Sheriff Romulo Martinez fearing that the four desperate men, the Kid, Rudabaugh, Billy Wilson and (Edward M.) Kelly, would ere long make a desperate effort to

get out, had promised to pay one of the prisoners if he would assist the guard in keeping watch, and yesterday the fellow informed him that the men were trying to dig out. Sheriff Martinez, accompanied by Deputy Marshall Neis, at once proceeded to the jail, and entering the cell, found the men at supper. They examined the room and found that the bed ticking was filled with stones and earth, and removing the mattress discovered a deep hole. Further investigation showed that the men had dug themselves nearly out, and by concealing the loose earth in the bed and covering the hole up with it had almost reached the street without awakening the suspicion of the guard. Last night they were closely guarded and heavily ironed, and today further precautions will be taken.

Afraid of vigilante action in Las Vegas, Rudabaugh requested a trial in Santa Fe. On April 22 a Santa Fe court found him guilty of murder and sentenced him to hang in Las Vegas on May 20. Rudabaugh immediately appealed his sentence. The authorities sent him to the Las Vegas County jail to await the results.

In September, still waiting for his appeal trial, Rudabaugh attempted to escape jail by picking the lock. The attempt failed when he awoke one of the guards asleep in the hallway.

Then, on the morning of December 3, 1881, the guards discovered that seven prisoners had escaped through a nineteen-by-seventeen-inch hole in the stone wall of one of the cells. After almost a year of incarceration, Dave Rudabaugh and his friend J. J. Webb were free. That morning Rudabaugh and Webb hopped a train and left Las Vegas. Four months later, Webb died of smallpox in Winslow, Arkansas.

Five years later Dirty Dave was working and walking the streets of Hidalgo de Parral, Mexico. The town suited him. It was at the end of Chihuahua, a barren, hilly, rugged place that even Mother Nature seemed to distain. What made it a town at all was the silver that had been discovered and was being mined in the surrounding hills. Silver brought life to the village—as well as brothels, cantinas, and gaming halls. These in turn brought unsavory characters into town, including Dirty Dave, who began making his living at the card tables.

His disposition and his dishevelment hadn't improved in his five years in Hidalgo de Parral. If anything, he was more unpleasant and dirtier. He insulted everyone, abused the Mexicans, and was a dangerous man to challenge.

On February 18, 1886, he was at his usual station playing cards at the cantina. Although he did not understand Spanish, he did know that the natives were being particularly insulting and obnoxious. One of the players suddenly stood, and reaching for his pistol, accused Dirty Dave of cheating. Rudabaugh shot him right between the eyes. Another player took a shot at him but missed, and Rudabaugh proceeded to plug him through the heart. No one in the cantina paid much attention to the gunfight, since it was not an unusual occurrence.

Rudabaugh had had enough for the night. He left the cantina and went for his horse—but it was nowhere in sight. Cursing a blue streak, Rudabaugh headed back to a now-darkened cantina. The street around him was strangely deserted and barricaded.

Rudabaugh knew then that he was a marked man. All his senses went on alert, and he pulled out his gun and cautiously continued toward the cantina. But for all his caution, the life of Dirty Dave Rudabaugh—the man no jail could hold, a member of Billy the Kid's gang, and a feared outlaw—was coming to an end. "Come out and fight," he roared to the night. His answer was a rifle shot, then another, and another. "Coward!" he screamed—and fell dead.

Townspeople poured into the street. Legend has it that one man wielded a sword and neatly severed Dirty Dave's head from his body. For hours the head was paraded around the town. Then, the crowd went to the cemetery, dug a hole, and dumped in the head and body.

The dirtiest outlaw came to a dirty end: a bundle of bones, blood, and dirt in a shallow, unconsecrated grave.

Milton Yarberry
A Shootin' Fool

Harry Brown considered himself a rather important man about town. In 1881 he played a minor part in thwarting a train robbery attempt by Dave Rudabaugh and Dave Mather. Although his role was insignificant, he played it up as the main reason the robbery failed. He was overly self-confident and filled with bravado.

To add to his elevated self-esteem, his father and his uncle were former governors of Tennessee. There were not many in the Old West that could lay claim to such distinguished family ties. However, Brown's family background did little to make him a gentleman. He was a hard drinker, always looking for an argument or, better yet, a fight, and was quick to pull a gun. So what happened to Harry on the evening of March 27, 1881, came as no surprise.

On this night in March, a pleased Harry dismounted from a hack in front of Girard's Restaurant in Albuquerque, extended his hand to the lovely Sadie Preston, and escorted her into the restaurant. Because of his self-conceived image, he had no doubt that he would succeed in wooing Sadie. A few moments later Brown came out and stood in front of the restaurant, looking as though he was waiting for someone.

As Brown stood outside the restaurant, John Clark, the hack driver, spotted the town constable, Milton Yarberry, walking toward the restaurant holding the hand of Sadie's four-year-old daughter. Clark knew that Milton Yarberry and Harry Brown were competing for Sadie's attention, and he thought it was a bit brazen of Mrs. Preston to let Yarberry take care of her child while she went out for the evening with his rival. Clark, however, had learned that in the West, questions or speculation could get

In Memory
of
MILTON
YARBERY
Died Feb. 9, 1883
Rest in peace.

Erected by
Robert A. Hat...

A loser in life and in death: Milton Yarberry's grave marker with his name misspelled

Image from Deadly Dozen © 2003 by Robert K. DeArment, Courtesy University of Oklahoma Press

you in serious trouble, especially with gunslingers, outlaws, and lawmen. Moreover, because he was a black man, he found it best to keep his opinions to himself.

The driver couldn't help but notice the remarkable contrast between Brown and Yarberry. Whereas Brown's look was distinguished, Yarberry's could be called distinctive—at best. He was thirty-three years old and had slightly stooped shoulders and a tall, lanky body. His neck was exceptionally long and supported a too-small head covered with dark hair and adorned with a dark mustache. His six-foot-three frame and his long neck made him look like he was rushing forward, even though his gait was always slow and loping.

Everything about Yarberry's features created a cold and cunning appearance—from his too-thin nose to his mouth with its cruel twist, to his dull gray eyes that constantly shifted, never looking too long at anything or anyone.

Yarberry's upbringing also contrasted sharply with the wealthy Brown's. According to Yarberry, he was born in Walnut Grove, Arkansas, in 1849. He said he left Arkansas for Texas when his family was involved in a killing over a land dispute. Newspapers had a different take on his early years, reporting that he left because he was wanted for murder in Sharp, Arkansas. In Texas he was a Ranger; after that, he operated a saloon and billiard parlor.

In 1878 the citizens of Canon City, Colorado, chased him out of town for operating a dishonest saloon. Yarberry set up another saloon and variety theater in the Colorado Territory with Tony Preston, who was to become the divorced husband of Sadie.

When Yarberry left Colorado and his business with Preston, he operated brothels in a series of railroad towns with a female a partner called "Steamboat." Las Vegas, New Mexico Territory, was one of the towns where he set up shop. However, he left that town in a hurry when he was suspected of robbing and killing a freighter.

In 1881 he arrived in Albuquerque and won the job of constable, although his character and past hardly suited him for the job. When Yarberry's name appeared on the ballot for the position, the only thing voters knew about him was that he was an experienced gunman. Apparently, that was the only qualification he needed. Milt beat his opponent, J. H. Robb, by a landslide with a vote of fifty-five to nineteen. Yarberry's victory did not come as a total surprise, however. Robb was a write-in candidate; Yarberry's name was the only one printed on the ballot.

Now here was the new constable, walking down the street with Sadie's daughter, heading for the restaurant where Clark was parked. Yarberry entered the restaurant with the child, but emerged a few minutes later, alone. He joined the waiting Brown.

As the men headed for an empty lot down the street, they passed Clark, who overheard Brown say, "Milt, I want you to understand I am not afraid of you and would not be even if you were marshal of the United States." Clark figured Yarberry had threatened Brown with his position as town constable.

The driver turned away from the men but spun around a few minutes later when he heard shots. He saw Brown stagger as Yarberry shot him in the chest. Then Yarberry pumped two more shots into Brown as he lay sprawled on the sidewalk.

Accused of murder, Yarberry insisted it was self-defense. "When they reached the empty lot," Yarberry reported, "Brown used some of the vilest language he could lay his tongue to. He was, I could see, trying hard to get the drop on me."

Yarberry continued his story, saying he had his back to the restaurant when he heard Sadie call to Brown:

I did not look around and a moment later Brown struck me a blow in the face with his left hand, at the same time drawing his six-shooter with his right, and immediately firing his first shot, grazing

51

my right hand and inflicting a trifling scratch on the thumb. In an instant I realized that I must either kill him or die, and quicker than it takes to tell, I whipped out my gun and began firing.

This testimony described a brave man fighting a vile man, and the jury was convinced. Milt Yarberry was acquitted on a verdict of self-defense.

Some townsfolk were not satisfied with the verdict. Many believed Yarberry murdered Brown to clear a path in his pursuit of Sadie Preston. In May 1882 pressure from locals led a grand jury to indict Yarberry for murder. Again, witnesses declared that they had heard Brown threaten Milt. The plea was again self-defense, and on May 19, the grand jury found Yarberry innocent of the charges.

The acquittal seemed to prove to Yarberry that he was important and powerful as constable and that he had the right to shoot when he deemed it necessary. That assumption ended in Yarberry making a fatal mistake. A wise man would have lain low, but Yarberry was anything but wise. He was a shootin' fool, and it took him less than a month to prove it.

On a June 18, 1881, Milt was relaxing in front of his friend Elwood Maden's house. The house faced the main street in town. He and "Monte" Frank Boyd were deep in conversation when they heard the crack of a gun. The sound came from down the street, in the vicinity of the Greenleaf restaurant. The two headed for the restaurant, and as they approached, they saw a man hurrying down the street.

Yarberry asked who fired the shot, and a bystander pointed to the fleeing figure. Yarberry and Boyd chased after him. "Stop there, I want you!" yelled Yarberry.

There are as many versions of what happened next as there were eyewitnesses, but all agree on one thing: Charles C. Campbell, the man fleeing down the street, soon lay dead, killed by three bullets fired by Yarberry and Boyd.

After the Campbell incident, Yarberry immediately surrendered to Sheriff Perfecto Armijo. The newspapers went to work, publishing sensational headlines such as the one from a Santa Fe paper declaring, "Great excitement prevails in Albuquerque."

Sheriff Armijo locked up Yarberry, but couldn't find Boyd, who was last seen boarding a westbound train. Sixteen months later, a band of Navajos hunted down and killed Boyd after he murdered an unarmed tribesman.

The story Yarberry gave the sheriff about the Campbell shooting was predictable. He stated that he and Boyd had heard a shot and had gone to investigate. Boyd asked someone who had done the shooting, and a man said, "There he goes," pointing to the retreating Campbell. According to Yarberry, he told the man to stop and hold up his hands; instead, Campbell pulled out his pistol and shot at him.

Although Yarberry claimed that he told Campbell to halt and that Campbell turned and shot at him, the physicians attending to the body of Campbell had a different story. Their examination showed that Campbell had three bullet holes in his back. Witnesses reported that Yarberry kept firing, even after Campbell fell to the ground.

Campbell's funeral drew a huge crowd. Almost the entire male population of Albuquerque attended. The mood was ugly, and there was talk of a lynching.

A hearing on July 5 ordered Yarberry held for the grand jury. Sheriff Armijo, judging the mood of the town crowd to be hostile and not having a safe jail in Albuquerque, took the prisoner to Santa Fe for safekeeping to await his Bernalillo County grand jury appearance.

Almost a year later, on May 11, the grand jury met and determined that Yarberry would stand trial for murder at the district court. Meanwhile, Yarberry was to remain in the safe and secure custody of the Santa Fe jail.

The trial took three days. Yarberry claimed self-defense, but the jury returned a guilty verdict. The most damning evidence came from

Thomas W. Parks, a Nebraska attorney, who testified that he saw Yarberry shoot Campbell in the back after he stopped and held up his empty hands.

Yarberry stuck to his story, declaring that after he yelled at Campbell to stop, the man spun around and began shooting. He testified, "As soon as he began firing at me I returned it without much delay. I only hit him once. The other shots were fired by Boyd, who was some yards to my left and the bullets from his six-shooter struck Campbell in the back. My shot struck him in the right side." Yarberry insisted he hit Campbell with only the one bullet. "I killed him, or shot at him—for no one knows whether my shot or Boyd's killed him, because I know he meant to kill me."

In less than ten minutes, the jury returned a verdict of murder in the first degree. Yarberry was to hang on June 16. His defense lawyers immediately filed an appeal to the New Mexico Supreme Court, and Yarberry was sent back to the Santa Fe jail to wait. It would be a long one. The Supreme Court would not meet until January 1883, two years after the shooting of Campbell.

By September 1882 Yarberry had had enough of jail life. He escaped on September 9 with a holdup man, a wife murderer, and a counterfeiter. The escapees filed through their shackles, tossed a blanket over the guard's head, then tied him up. One of the foursome was quickly captured, but the others made it out of town. Yarberry's freedom lasted only three days, however. He was captured by Frank Chevez, Santa Fe police chief, twenty-eight miles from town.

Yarberry returned to jail a despondent man who complained bitterly about "having all the world against [him] and being hunted like a wild animal." He tried to keep his spirits up by drinking a bottle of whiskey a day. He confided to Santa Fe Sheriff Martinez that "whiskey is all that keeps me up. I would break down without it."

On January 25, 1883, the final word came down. The Supreme Court refused to reverse his death penalty. Governor Sheldon immediately issued a death warrant, and Sheriff Armijo started the preparations for Yarberry's hanging. The sheriff was instructed by the authorities to take Yarberry "to some safe and convenient place" and hang him between the hours of eleven a.m. and three p.m. on February 9, 1883.

Armijo made careful preparations for the hanging of Yarberry. For some unknown reason, he was fond of the man and did not wish him to suffer. He chose an inch-and-half rope and carefully soaked and stretched it. Yarberry was to be hanged by a new method called the "jerk plan." Rather than having a trapdoor spring open beneath his feet, he would be jerked upward with a series of pulleys and ropes anchored by a four-hundred-pound weight. When the short rope to the anchor was cut, Yarberry would be hurled upward with such force that his neck would snap.

The sheriff, for whatever reason, decided to make the hanging an event. Perhaps he wanted to do Yarberry honor, or perhaps he wanted to set an example. He sent out a hundred invitations to view the hanging. Locals living near the hanging site rented out their rooftops at a dollar per person to spectators without the special invitation. Yarberry would go out with a spectacular showing attended by almost a thousand witnesses.

Yarberry's road to death started at dawn on February 9. A detachment from the New Mexico militia escorted him to the train station. When he arrived in Albuquerque, fifteen hundred people greeted him. Another group of militia took custody of him and took him to the jail. Friends came to say goodbye and brought Yarberry a new black suit to replace the tatty brown one he had been wearing.

On the day of his hanging, Yarberry contacted the local priests and asked to be baptized into the Catholic faith. Having taken care of his mortal soul, he took care of his mortal body by requesting cranberry pie, a pint of whiskey, and a bottle of ale for his last meal.

Elwood Maden was one of Yarberry's friends who came to visit and say good-bye. Yarberry confessed to Maden that he had been in some trouble before coming to Albuquerque, but that he had never killed anyone. He admitted that his name was not Yarberry or Johnson, a name he went by in Texas. He confessed that he did not use his real name because he wanted to protect his respectable parents. Although that is a plausible story, Yarberry hardly had the moral conscience for that kind of an act.

As the clock rang a quarter to three, Yarberry, attired in his nice black suit and with his arms secured to his sides, left the jail and shuffled between the ranks formed by the militia. He mounted the scaffold and stood there with his legs bound and the thick noose around his neck.

Sheriff Armijo asked Yarberry if he had any last words. Yarberry started his verbal ramblings with reference to the Brown shooting, and he seemed to address himself as he spoke. "Well, Milt," he began, "they are going to hang you because you killed a son of Governor Brown of Tennessee." He went on: "Several of my friends told me he had made threats on my life and wanted to kill me and told me to keep out of his way. I told them I didn't want no row with Brown but I wasn't going to hide from him or keep in any back rooms out of his sight. When I did kill him I did it in defense of my life and I was tried and acquitted, but they are determined to hang Milt and they are going to do it." Milt went on to lecture his audience about the Campbell shooting and his innocence. "He shot me and I shot back."

Yarberry managed to ramble on for almost fifteen minutes. Armijo's orders were to hang the prisoner by three o'clock in the afternoon. As the bell tolled three, Armijo snapped shut his watch, and nodded to Count Epur, a local character and assigned executioner, who swung the axe cutting the rope that held the weight.

Milton Yarberry shot straight up in the air, his head hit the crossbar, and his body dropped down and hung there, slowly swaying back and forth. At nine minutes after three o'clock, Milton Yarberry was pronounced dead. His body, with the noose still attached, was placed in a plain wooden coffin and buried in the Catholic cemetery.

Milt Yarberry was a poorly educated, brutal, and uncouth man. A reporter once stated that he lacked the mentality to distinguish between a legal act and an unlawful one. These traits, combined with his belief that he was always right and that others were after him, made him a shootin' fool and led to his swinging at the end of a rope.

Billy the Kid
The Killing of the Kid

Billy the Kid is on the run, living in his saddle, and hiding out with some of the sheepherders around Fort Sumner. He's begging for meals—but there is never enough to eat. It's late evening, July 13, 1881, and a hungry and saddlesore Billy rides into Fort Sumner to see his lover and to spend some time with his Mexican friends at the fort. Near midnight he rolls out of bed, not bothering to put on his shoes. Pete Maxwell has butchered a steer, and beef sounds mighty appealing to the hungry Kid. Off the table he grabs his six-shooter and picks up a butcher knife to cut himself a steak.

In stocking feet he pads across the porch to Maxwell's bedroom for the key to the meat locker. He passes two strangers sitting on the edge of the porch near the doorway to Maxwell's room, open to catch the evening breeze. Billy wonders who the men are and what they are doing at Maxwell's Fort Sumner house. *"Quiénes son usted?"* he asks them—who are you? *"Amigos,"* they reply.

Although they identify themselves as friends, his concern about the strangers grows. He slips past them and enters Maxwell's bedroom. As he enters the room, he turns and approaches the bed, softly questioning, "Who are the men outside, Pete? Who are they?" Maxwell doesn't answer.

Sheriff Pat Garrett is sitting next to Maxwell's bed, but the deep shadows of the room hide him from Billy's sight. Garrett sees the slim figure as it enters the darkened room. When he hears the voice, he knows he has his man. Garrett makes a slight move for his gun. Perhaps Billy sees the movement, or perhaps he senses that someone besides Maxwell is in the room. Instinctively he steps back, but he doesn't shoot, even though he has his six-gun in hand. That hesitation costs Billy his life.

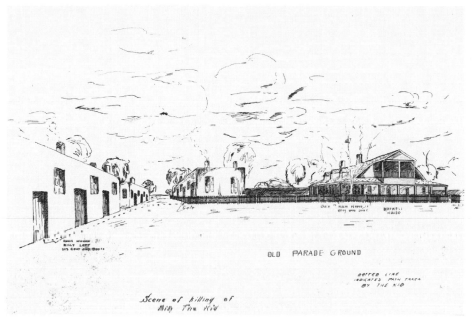

A sketch of the Maxwell House at Fort Sumner showing Billy the Kid's route on the night he was killed

Courtesy Palace of the Governors (MNM/DCA), #51240

Garrett quickly snaps off a shot that throws Billy's body to the side. Billy lurches backward and falls. Garrett's first shot hits Billy in the chest; his second hits the wall. Then Garrett hears the moan. In the grip of terror, he runs from the room, followed by Pete Maxwell. "I've just killed Billy the Kid," he shouts. "I've killed him."

Deputies Kip McKinney and John Poe are waiting outside on the porch. Garrett explains to them what happened, but the men doubt that the infamous Kid is actually dead. To prove it, Maxwell gets a candle and holds it up to the bedroom window. There on the floor, in the flickering candlelight, the deputies see the body. It is the first time they have ever actually seen Billy the Kid. McKinney is a New Mexico man, and Poe is a cattle detective for the Canadian River Cattlemen's Association who has recently been deputized by Garrett.

A crowd of locals, drawn by the gunshots, begins gathering around the ranch house. Deputy McKinney enters the bedroom and sees a woman cradling the body. When Garrett reenters the room, he finds McKinney kneeling next to her.

Many of the Mexicans living at the fort are friends of Billy's. With real sorrow, they begin to remove the body and prepare it for burial. Gently they carry it across the street to a carpenter's shop. Billy the Kid is laid out on a long, simple wooden table while the carpenter builds his coffin.

One of the local men in the crowd is Justice of the Peace Alejandro Saguaro. He gathers several men together and informs them they are now a coroner's jury. However, before the jury can view the body, Garrett writes a report and thrusts it into the hands of the jury members, telling them to sign it. They do so and return the paper to Garrett.

The following day, Milnor Rudulph rides into Sumner to report the death. Another coroner's jury is formed. This jury supposedly views the body, writes out a report in Spanish, and gives it to Garrett to be filed.

That afternoon, the Kid is buried in the fort's cemetery next to his friends and fellow outlaws, Tom O'Folliard and Charles Bowdre.

Garrett had begun his search for Billy the Kid three months before that July night, but the trail had turned cold and Garrett had become discouraged. He became increasing convinced that Billy had run for the Mexican border.

It wasn't a whim that sent Garrett to Pete Maxwell's ranch house to track Billy. It was a lead from John Poe. Poe had heard talk from old friends that Billy the Kid was hanging around Fort Sumner. Rumor had it that Billy had a Mexican girlfriend there, and Sheriff Garrett was willing to follow any lead.

He and his deputies rode into Fort Sumner that night of July 13, 1881, to question Pete Maxwell about Billy's whereabouts. Garrett figured that as a friend, Maxwell would cooperate and give him information on Billy.

Garrett and the two deputies arrived outside Maxwell's house about nine o'clock at night. They hid in the peach orchard for several hours, waiting for another deputy. About midnight they decided their wait was futile, and the three approached the house. Garrett told his deputies to remain outside while he checked with Maxwell. The deputies positioned themselves near the rail that ran around the porch

Billy the Kid was no stranger to Garrett. During the Lincoln County War days, Garrett and Billy had been friends. Garrett spent a considerable amount of time in Lincoln at the gaming tables, where he met and frequently played poker with the Kid. Kid was nicknamed Little Casino; Pat, who was over six feet tall, Big Casino. After they left Lincoln they went their separate ways. Garrett cleaned up and became a law enforcer, while Billy continued his lawlessness.

During his outlaw career Billy the Kid had been captured and jailed but escaped. While breaking out of jail, he killed two deputies; afterwards, Lew Wallace, the governor of New Mexico Territory, offered a $500 reward for his capture. Garrett, a new sheriff in the territory, was seeking to make a name for himself; that and the lure of $500 made him determined to end the career of the infamous outlaw.

Six days after Garrett shot the Kid, he rode into Santa Fe to claim the reward from acting Governor W. G. Ritch (Governor Wallace had left New Mexico to accept a post as the U.S. ambassador to Turkey). Ritch wanted to look over the records pertaining to the reward before paying. On July 23 Ritch informed Garrett that he would not pay the reward. He claimed it was a personal offer made by the former governor, and the territory was not bound to honor it.

People around the state begin raising money to reward Garrett. On August 6, Garrett was given $1,300 by the residents of Dona Ana County and $600 by Santa Fe County. Finally, in 1882, Pat was awarded $500 from New Mexico Territory.

But not everyone believed that Pat Garrett's action was an act of justice; some saw it as cold-blooded murder. And indeed, the shooting was not the result of a chase, a gunfight, a challenge, or even an attempted capture. In shooting Billy the Kid, it was believed that Garrett had violated the *duello*—one of the unwritten codes of the Old West. The duello mandated that gunfighters either warn their victims or give them a chance to draw before firing. Garrett did neither.

Garrett may have convinced himself that he was ridding the people of a dangerous villain. But at the time of the shooting, more than 60 percent of the territory's citizens considered Billy a hero and a victim, not a villain. And they now believed that their hero, their icon of the Old West, had been murdered—killed without a fighting chance. But had he been?

Deputy Kip McKinney, who accompanied Sheriff Garrett to the fort that night, didn't think so. He told a different story about the night the Kid was killed. McKinney's story matches Garrett's—except, according to McKinney, Billy hadn't been killed. He believed that Billy survived his gunshot wound, and that a man who had died the night before, a Mexican, was buried at the fort in place of Billy the Kid.

Although the two deputies believed Garrett when he told them that the man lying dead was Billy the Kid, they later changed their minds and maintained that the Kid had lived. And the deputies weren't the only old westerners who believed that Billy had survived. A man named Collins said he helped carry the body that Garrett claimed was Billy the Kid to the grave, but he insisted it was not actually Billy. Caesar Brock, an acquaintance of both Billy and Garrett, said that they killed a Mexican and buried him, pretending that he was the Kid. And rumor has it that Billy roamed around New Mexico Territory for a long time after his supposed death. Some say he traveled from ranch to ranch looking for work, never saying who he was or from where he hailed. Eventually, he headed for Mexico with his lover.

But if Billy the Kid was not killed on the night of July 13, why would Pete Maxwell, Pat Garrett, and the Mexicans who lived at the fort go along with the hoax? Publicly, Garrett insisted on the truth of his story and hired Marshall Ashmum Upson to write a book about the event, entitled *An Authentic Life of Billy the Kid.* The book, filled with lies and half-truths, was an abysmal failure for Garrett. Interestingly, there is no record of Pete Maxwell's account of that night. And Garrett never filed any of the coroner's jury findings.

Money is always a great motivator, and $500 in the 1800s was a considerable amount for anyone, including a sheriff. Also, it has been suggested that Billy's girlfriend was actually related to Garrett and Maxwell. Perhaps the reward and family ties were enough for Garrett and Maxwell to fake Billy's death. As for the residents of Fort Sumner, Billy was a good friend to the Mexicans at the fort. For him they would keep their silence.

As for Garrett his life was never easy after the incident. He was known as "the man who killed Billy the Kid." He lost a reelection for sheriff and was denied several other government appointments. He spent his late years on his New Mexico ranch fighting a running battle with goatherders, and his end came in a most inglorious way. In 1908 he was shot to death while relieving himself by the side of the road.

Over the years there have been attempts made to end the controversy over Billy the Kid's death. Most recently, in New Mexico, researchers planned to dig up the supposed graves of Billy the Kid and his mother and compare their DNA. Unfortunately, a flood at Fort Sumner in 1990 washed away the tombstones, making it uncertain which plot was Billy's, so the excavation never happened. And in 2006, Tom Sullivan, a former Lincoln County sheriff, and Steve Sederwall, who was once mayor of Capitan, New Mexico, dug up a grave in Prescott, Arizona, that they claimed was Billy the Kid's. They hoped to compare bone DNA with bloodstains on the table where Billy was laid out. Their attempt failed.

And so the debate goes on. Was Billy the Kid killed by Pat Garrett at Fort Sumner on July 13, 1881, or did the Kid escape? More than a hundred years later, there are still no definitive answers to the mystery of the death of Billy the Kid.

Joel Fowler

Hanged for the Wrong Reasons

Montague Stevens of the Stevens–Upcher Ranch was enjoying a pleasant evening sitting outside the Grand Central Hotel in Socorro with friends. November 8, 1883, was a balmy night, and a soft breeze lazily swirled cigar smoke over the heads of the four men.

Suddenly the quiet evening was interrupted by the sound of a ruckus coming from the barroom inside the hotel. The men rushed to the front window of the hotel and saw Joel Fowler spraying bullets around the feet of an old man. The elderly man was trying his best to avoid the bullets by doing a jig.

Tonight, Fowler was having a grand old time. He was rolling in dough and sloshing in liquor. Earlier, Fowler had banked $52,000 in the Socorro bank from the sale of his Alamo ranch. After depositing that considerable sum, Fowler and his wife, Josie, checked into the Socorro Grand Central Hotel. Then Fowler went out to celebrate.

Somewhere along Fowler's drinking route he was joined by James Cale, a traveling salesman. Someone introduced Fowler to Cale as an important cattleman in the country. Being new in town, Cale didn't know anything else about Fowler. If he had asked the citizens around town about his drinking partner, they would have told him that Joel was a nice enough fellow when he wasn't drinking, but a mean SOB when imbibing the brew. Maybe that knowledge would have saved him; or maybe destiny had already dictated that night's events.

Fowler and Cale were well into their cups before their arrival at the Grand Central Hotel bar. To Cale, Fowler was a good drinking partner. However, when Fowler started waving his six-shooter around and forcing

Joel Fowler, one of the vilest outlaws of the Old West
© J. E. Smith Collection

the old man to dance, Cale became concerned. He suggested that he and Fowler have another drink and leave the old man alone.

Through the hotel window, Montague saw Fowler put his six-shooter on the bar and reach for his drink. He also saw Cale signal the barkeeper to take Fowler's gun and stash it behind the bar. Unfortunately, Fowler also saw Cale's signal. What happened next started out as a shouting match.

"Give me back my gun," Fowler yelled at the barkeeper.

The barkeeper, hoping to cool the situation and avoid trouble, told Fowler that he would give him back his gun in the morning. That seemed to inflame Fowler's temper even more. The onlookers witnessed Fowler whip around, glare at Cale, and bellow, "It was you that told him to take my six-shooter. Take this." And with that Fowler lurched at Cale, striking him a slight blow.

Montague and his friends did not see Fowler go for his penknife. But they did see Cale crumple on the ground, his chest spurting blood.

The four observers rushed into the bar. Montague and another man grabbed Fowler's arms. A third man took one look at Cale and ran for the sheriff.

Fowler struggled against Montague's hold and fought to bite the hand restraining him. Montague turned Fowler's arm and warned him, "If you try to bite me, I'll twist your arm off."

Sheriff Simpson rushed into the bar. He knelt next to Cale, who was heaped on the floor. The sheriff saw Fowler being restrained by two determined men. There wasn't much of an explanation needed to sort out the details. With the help of several men, Sheriff Simpson dragged Fowler off to the Socorro jail and delivered Cale to the doctor's office.

Montague and his pals found out later that Fowler had struck Cale with a penknife that entered Cale's chest just below the left nipple, making a half-inch-wide wound. The force of Fowler's lurching toward Cale caused the knife to go deep and nick the edge of Cale's heart sac.

For three days Cale lingered. Although he was coherent, his case was hopeless, and he knew it. The seepage from his heart could not be stopped, and on November 11, Cale died from his wound.

Joel Fowler was charged with murder. And it was soon discovered that this wasn't the first time he had killed. While he was in jail for Cale's murder, a second warrant for Fowler was issued. This one was for the murder of Poney Deal and William "Butcher Knife" Childs.

The murders of Deal and Childs were a melodramatic crime of true Wild West proportions. The saga began the previous year, 1882, when Fowler killed three of his hired hands, including one named Forrest, for rustling his cattle. At that time in the West, rustling was considered a legitimate reason to kill a man. When Fowler hired Deal to cowboy on his Alamo Ranch, he had no idea that Deal was Forrest's brother.

In September Fowler returned to his ranch after searching for stray horses and discovered that Deal had threatened a ranch hand. That's when he learned of the relationship between Deal and the deceased Forrest.

Fowler paid Deal off, and, according to Fowler, their parting was amicable. Deal announced he was heading for Texas, but instead he headed for Socorro and joined his friend "Butcher Knife" Bill Childs. Together they set out for Fowler's ranch, intending to kill him.

Fowler and a few hands were on their way to the Alamo Ranch when they met Deal and Childs at a place called the Stone House. A gun battle ensued and ended with Childs being killed and Deal ducking into the house. When McGee, the owner of the Stone House, arrived, he yelled at Deal, demanding that he leave his house. There was no response. McGee went to the door and kicked it in. He poked his head inside and was met by a blast from Deal's gun that killed him instantly.

Deal refused to leave the Stone House the rest of that day. As dawn broke, Fowler ordered his hands to set fire to the house. The roof caught on fire first, and smoke began billowing into the rooms. A single shot was heard, then nothing. When the men were able to search the ruins, they found Deal's body. Rather than face Fowler and justice, it appeared that Deal had committed suicide.

For some twisted reason, it was generally accepted that Deal's death was Fowler's fault. Trusting in his innocence, Fowler turned himself into Sheriff Simpson after the incident and gave his side of the story. The next day he was tried and acquitted.

But now, with another killing attributed to Fowler, the mood of the town swung. So while Fowler was in jail another warrant was issued; this one, for the murders of Deal and Butcher Knife.

Fowler's character fell under a dark cloud of suspicion. Previous rumors hinted that Fowler's cattle herd had a way of growing in direct proportion to the shrinking of his neighbors' herds, and that Fowler's cowhands seem to disappear just before payday. There was also talk that Fowler would sometimes sell his cattle and then steal them back. The persistent rumors lingered, although they were never proven.

Fowler's background may have contributed to his peculiar personality and dangerous behavior. Joel Fowler was born in Indiana in 1849 of well-educated and respected parents. His education was complete enough for him to quote Shakespeare whenever he was in a profound mood.

In the 1870s Fowler traveled to Fort Worth and lived with his uncle, a senator in the Texas legislature. Perhaps his connection to politics made him think he was invincible to the law. He led an honest life until the day he caught his beautiful young wife in bed with another man. He shot the lover and hightailed it out of Texas, showing up in Las Vegas, New Mexico, in the summer of 1879.

At the time, Las Vegas was booming. The Atchison, Topeka, and Santa Fe Railroad had just come into town, and Fowler astutely opened a dance hall and variety theater near the depot.

Not long after the opening of the dance hall, he married Josie, one of his dancers, described by a Santa Fe newspaper as "his equal in grit and general cussedness." Six months later the couple moved to Santa Fe, and Fowler opened the Texas Saloon.

On February 27, 1880, Fowler was the subject of an article in the *Santa Fe New Mexican*. The article depicted Joel as a man who was like-able—except when he was drinking. One of Joel's more consistent drunken behaviors was to aimlessly shoot up the town. He'd shoot at the sun, at water tanks, and down the street, regardless of whether it was occupied or not. That behavior earned him a few stays in the town jail, and in one case a lullaby sung by a jailer who hoped to calm Fowler down.

Leaving Las Vegas, Joel and Josie moved to White Oaks, a gold and silver mining town in Lincoln County, New Mexico Territory, where they opened up another saloon. On May 31, 1880, two drunks began shooting up the town. Fowler figured it was his duty to intervene, and he shot and killed them both. The town considered that Fowler was just doing his civic duty, and he was never charged with a crime.

The saloon business was good to the Fowlers, and in 1881 Joel was financially able to establish his Alamo Ranch, a cattle ranch in Socorro County a hundred miles northwest of White Oaks, near the railhead of Magdalena. It was on this ranch that Fowler caught Deal's brother and two other ranch hands rustling his stock and killed them.

After the Cale murder, it seemed that all of Fowler's sins were catching up to him. As he waited in the Socorro jail, the Committee of Safety was conducting clandestine meetings on his fate.

The Committee of Safety was the grandiose name for the Socorro vigilantes. They had been organized by Colonel Ethan Eaton after the murder of his friend, publisher Anthony M. Conklin, went unpunished.

Conklin was shot leaving church on Christmas Eve by three young members of the Baca family. The murder took place in full view of the departing congregation, and although the killers were identified by several witnesses, they went unpunished. Law officials of Mexican decent were known for placing family loyalty above justice, and Constable Juan Maria Garcia was a close relative of the Baca family. The fact that nothing was done to apprehend the Baca men and bring them to justice infuriated Eaton. He decided that it was time the citizens took justice into their own hands, and the Committee of Safety was formed.

Eaton started by calling a series of meetings in and around Socorro, imploring town residents to take responsibility for cleaning up their town and restoring law and order. On January 1, 1881, the Socorro Committee of Safety became official when a notice was published in the *Socorro Sun* announcing that all violators of peace and good order would meet speedy and sure punishment by the committee.

Membership in the Committee of Safety was almost mandatory for the Anglos living in and around Socorro. Eaton pressured the Anglo townspeople, especially its town's leading citizens, to join, implying that not joining was tantamount to not wanting a lawful town. The group's membership rapidly grew and soon included businessmen, doctors, lawyers, bankers, the editor of the local paper, two reverends, and law enforcement officers.

Although the Committee of Safety was not sanctioned by any law enforcement agency, it acted like the law. It was highly structured, with officers, dues, procedures for scheduled and emergency meetings, and a chairman, Eaton, who kept a diary of the committee's business. And its members acted swiftly if they felt that the town's actual lawmen were moving too slowly or if it looked as though an outlaw might escape punishment. In those cases, the committee pursued the criminals in question and hanged them—proving itself to be nothing more than a vigilante outfit.

The committee members' first action came three months after the group was organized: They strung up Tom Gordon for killing the town marshal. By the time Joel Fowler was accused of killing James Cale, the Committee of Safety was well experienced in handling justice in Socorro.

On November 11, the day after Cale died, a jury was summoned by Judge Beall to decide the charge against Fowler for the Cale attack. A panel of six men viewed the body of Cale; heard testimonies from the post mortem examiners, Dr. Davis, Dr. Duncan, and Dr. Provost; and visited the crime scene at the Grand Central Hotel.

The doctors' reports stated that Cale died from a stab wound and that the instrument entered the left breast just below the left nipple, struck the fifth rib, and pricked the apex of the heart, causing internal hemorrhaging. Witnesses testified that they saw Fowler stab Cale.

The next day, after the panel reported, Justice of the Peace W. N. Beall formerly charged Fowler with the murder of James E. Cale. Josie Fowler was with her husband, quietly sitting next to him during the proceedings. Fowler was remanded to the Socorro jail without bail to await trial.

While Fowler was awaiting trial, a guard happened to check on him and discovered he was digging his way out of the jail. A horse was found nearby saddled and ready to ride. A revolver was also found hidden under his bed. Some reported that a man by the name of Tex had provided the revolver. Others said that Mrs. Fowler had delivered the revolver and a rope to her husband. There was also talk that Fowler had instructed someone to send telegrams to his friends asking them to break him out of jail. One telegram was supposedly sent to Wyatt Earp.

These reports inflamed the residents of Socorro and made the Committee of Safety even more determined to monitor the Fowler trial. Governor Sheldon became concerned and suggested that a change of venue might be appropriate, or at least that Fowler should be taken to Santa Fe and locked up for his own safety. That suggestion prompted an angry editorial from the city editor of the local paper, who demanded that the venue not be changed and insisted that Socorro could take care of its own in a fair and just manner.

The case came to trial on December 8, 1883. Fowler hired two lawyers to defend him: Tomas Catron of Santa Fe, for $5,000, and local lawyer, Neil B. Field. A jury of twelve Mexicans was selected. None of them spoke English; only five could read; and fewer could write. This peculiar composition might have been arranged by the committee, who wanted Fowler punished. It could also have been a political move. Since law enforcement had been taken out of the hands of the town's Mexican population, selecting Mexicans for jury duty could have been done to make them feel involved in the process. Sitting on a jury was not a prestigious position in the Old West, and Anglos tended to eschew it.

Catron's defense was based on Fowler's drunken state. He argued that Fowler was not in his right mind when the stabbing occurred. Therefore, he maintained, he was not guilty of premeditated murder, or murder one, which carried a mandatory penalty of death by hanging. Catron argued for murder four. He argued that Joel had not planned to murder Cale and that the killing was a passionate, mindless, and thoughtless action done by a man who was out of control due to inebriation.

Murder in the fourth degree was defined as "the killing of another in the heat of passion without a design to effect death by a dangerous weapon . . . " The difference and definitions between murder one and murder four were explained to the jury by Judge Jay Bell. He also

71

explained that fourth-degree murder carried the punishment of imprisonment for not more than seven years but not less than one, or a fine of at least $500. It did not carry the death penalty. The judge's explanations to the jury were made in English in the most formal of legal language—to a jury that spoke no English. It was left to the court translator to pass these instructions on to the Mexican jury. There is no record on how much of the judge's instructions or how much of the testimony was understood by the jury.

After hearing all of the testimony, the jury was sequestered the rest of the day and throughout the night. At ten o'clock the following morning, the jury filed into the courtroom and read its verdict. Fowler was found guilty of murder in the first degree. He was sentenced to hang on January 4, 1884.

Catron and Field demanded a new trial. They based their demand on the fact that when the prosecution asked for a first-degree murder conviction, the audience applauded. This, they believed, showed conclusively that Fowler could not get a fair trial in Socorro. They also filed an appeal to the Supreme Court, which was not scheduled to meet until after Fowler's execution date. Hearing this news, the Committee of Safety feared that the Supreme Court appeal might bring about Fowler's release.

The *Las Vegas Optic* fanned the flames by pointing out that Fowler might not get the punishment he deserved. The paper expressed the concern that the higher court would rule in favor of the lesser charge of murder four and that Fowler would escape death. The paper also pointed out that the Supreme Court would not meet until after January 1885 and that the citizens of Socorro would be paying for Fowler's care until then. Finally, the *Optic* suggested that Fowler meet Judge Lynch—a euphemism for a vigilante hanging.

Fowler's hanging date came and went. Catron's appeal was on the docket for the New Mexico Supreme Court.

On the evening of January 21, 1884, there was considerable activity around Socorro as the Committee of Safety gathered for a meeting.

Colonel Eaton recorded in his diary that night that committee members—
that is, vigilantes—relieved the militia guard at the jail but did nothing
more that night.

The following night at ten o'clock, the vigilantes met in closed ses-
sion. The next day the *Las Vegas Optic* reported the following.

> . . . a large body of men, all in mask, met in the outskirts of
> town, and there the arrangements which would send the soul of the
> murderer into eternity were perfected. The jail was visited about ten
> o'clock by one of the vigilantes and Fowler was found to be fast
> asleep. The guards, which had heretofore been surrounding the jail,
> had almost all been taken away and only a few men guarded the
> entrance to the outer door and two others paced up and down in the
> hallway. The vigilantes demanded that the guards leave quietly. Near
> 12:20 two hundred vigilantes, armed, masked, and determined
> approached the jail house door. Quietly and orderly. Colonel Eaton
> halted the delegation outside the door, the keys were obtained, all
> exits into Socorro were guarded, and none would leave or enter.

Montegue Stevens, who witnessed Fowler's attack on Cale, was also
a witness to what went on that night. He was in the Grand Central Hotel
when word came that Fowler was going to be lynched. Fowler was
dragged from the jail and taken down the road about a quarter mile
from the jail.

A large, sturdy cottonwood with a firm limb jutted out over the road
at a right angle. A large crowd ringed the tree. Stevens stood on the
fringes of the solid crowd, about 150 yards away from the tree. He saw
the men throw a rope around the tree. Then a man went up and tied the
rope to the limb, while another group of men held Fowler up. When the
rope was tied and placed around Fowler's neck, the men let him go.

The rope stretched, and Fowler's feet touched the ground. Someone
sent a man up the tree to shorten the rope, but Fowler's weight had tight-
ened the knot, and the man could not undo it.

Someone said, "Well never mind. We'll hang him anyway. Boys, let's get on Fowler." And with that about five men hung on him and added their weight. Thus Fowler didn't die by hanging, but by strangulation.

In his diary under January 22, 1884, Colonel Eaton noted that "Joel A. Fowler Cale murderer was hung by citizens about one o'clock am." Fowler's hanging was the last vigilante action in Socorro. The Committee of Safety believed that with the demise of Fowler, their mission had been accomplished. They had established justice in Socorro.

But the hanging did not end the fervor over Fowler. There were continual threats of revenge by his friends. And the hanging tree got a great deal of attention. For days, people would stop by to view the "death tree" and cut off pieces as souvenirs. A lawyer by the name of Tiffany lived across the street from the hanging site. So many people came to see the tree and stopped by his house to ask questions that he finally cut the tree down to gain some peace.

That may have ended the fascination with Fowler's hanging, but it doesn't answer the question of whether or not Fowler really committed first-degree murder and deserved to die. Was the killing of Cale unpremeditated, brought on by his severe state of drunkenness? It seems ironic that a man who brutally and with premeditation killed many men was finally hanged in punishment for an accident caused by drunkenness and a penknife. In hanging Fowler, perhaps the vigilante mob was not seeking fairness and justice, but looking to establish power and control in the lawless West.

Ada Hulmes

The Case of the Crazy Lover

The action in Silver City's Monarch Saloon was in full swing when Ada Hulmes and her roommate Claude Lewis arrived. Entering the saloon, Hulmes came to an abrupt stop, scanning the room crowded with men and a few females. Lewis headed for the bar, calling to Hulmes to join her for a drink. But Hulmes was not in a social mood, and her fierce expression advertised her feelings. She was on a mission—a blood mission.

She gave the room another quick scan. Apparently not finding what she was seeking, she turned, and with determination headed for the game room. It was there that she found her quarry. Lazily hanging around the gaming tables was Jack Brown, casually watching a game of cards.

Once she spotted Brown, Hulmes shouted that she was going to kill him. This threat caused heads to turn and brought conversations to a halt. Brown spun around and saw the gun that Hulmes was leveling at him. He immediately tried ducking behind a stove. Unfortunately, that was the wrong move. If Brown had tried to disarm Hulmes, the evening might have ended differently. But Jack was not known for his bravery.

Fueled by her fury, Hulmes snapped off a shot that caught Jack in his left side, plowed upward through his heart, and exited out the right side of his chest. With blood pouring from the bullet hole, Jack stumbled across the room and out the door. There his journey ended, and so did his life.

Meanwhile, Hulmes ran out the back door of the saloon, bumping into Savannah Randall. Savannah did laundry during the day but found other employment to keep her busy at night. She had heard the commotion in the saloon, and one look at Hulmes told her all she needed to know. Savannah grabbed Hulmes and quickly tucked her into one of the prostitution cribs behind the saloon.

Alerted by the sounds of shots and shouts in the saloon, Deputies Al Card and C. I. Cantle pushed their way through a rapidly expanding crowd that grew as news about the shooting raced through town. The deputies took one look around the saloon and headed out the back. Kicking in the door of the crib, they faced a wild Hulmes, who came at them swinging and yelling. The two deputies managed to subdue the crazed woman and drag her to jail.

What had prompted Hulmes to publicly commit this heinous crime? It was the age-old reason for murder: a scorned love. Playing the starring roles in this drama were two lovers: Ada Hulmes, the piano player at Silver City's Enterprise Saloon, and John V. "Jack" Brown, the local carpenter and fire chief.

It seems that Jack's relationship with Hulmes was cooling off. That was more than Hulmes could tolerate. Sensing his waning interest, she pleaded with him to spend an evening with her. She probably thought a romantic night would bring back Jack's affection. But Jack's interest was now engaged in another direction.

That night, a young man by the name of Henry Rosecrans delivered two messages from Jack—one to Hulmes and one to her roommate Claude Lewis. In Hulmes's message, Jack made his feelings very clear. He told her that he "wished to break off all familiarity."

That was a blow to love-struck Hulmes. What made it particularly bitter was the message in Jack's note to Claude, describing her as his new love interest.

After reading the note of rejection, a furious Hulmes jumped up, found her pistol, wrapped it in silk, and stuffed it down the front of her dress. She yelled to Claude to come with her, saying that she was "going to kill the son of a bitch."

"I'll not go with you if you are going to cause trouble," Claude told

The Santa Fe Penitentiary: Ada Hulmes's cell was located on the third floor; it was the cell reserved for women
Courtesy Palace of the Governors (MNM/DCA), #10223

Hulmes. Hulmes assuaged Claude's worries by assuring her that she wasn't going to hurt Jack, and the women left together for the Centennial.

Although Jack was Hulmes's lover, he was also the husband of a twenty-three-year-old wife and the father of a nineteen-month-old daughter and an infant son. These responsibilities seemed to have little impact on his behavior.

Brown was known for his loud suits and his overabundance of flashy jewelry. The local paper, the *Silver City Enterprise*, excused Jack's loud dress and flashy jewelry by blaming it on the rough frontier living he had experienced, attributing his lack of taste to his lack of exposure to sophisticated city life. The *Enterprise* article, written after his death, reported that Jack "had many faults yet was not a bad man." The newspaper also stated that Jack had "a warm heart and a generous hand."

Other papers had a different view on Hulmes, who was employed as a saloon piano player. One story written after the shooting described Hulmes as a "cold-blooded murderer," a fallen woman, and a bold adventuress; another called her a nymphomaniac.

Days after the crime, a heavily veiled Hulmes appeared before Justice Lucas to be arraigned. Later, Hulmes claimed that Justice Lucas was her first cousin. That information only fueled the high emotions of the Silver City citizens and increased their interest in the trial.

Sensing the mood of Silver City and the citizens' opinion of Hulmes, her attorneys, Idus L. Fielder and Gideon D. Bantz, requested a change of venue. The request was granted, and the trial was moved to Dona Ana County, a place known for its lenient juries.

Historically in the Old West women were rarely prosecuted or sentenced for crimes. As late as 1889 Silver City's Grant County was the only county that had sent a woman to the Santa Fe Penitentiary. That woman was Minnie Angel, who was found guilty of horse stealing. Soon after her sentencing, Minnie was pardoned. Hulmes's friends hoped that if found guilty, she too would be pardoned immediately, or at the worse, not be made to serve her whole sentence.

Hulmes's trial, which lasted for five days, began the first week in October 1889. There were well-known names on both sides of the case. William L. Rynerson and Edward C. Wade, district attorney for the third judicial district, were the prosecuting attorneys.

Rynerson had an interesting history. On December 15, 1867, he shot and killed John P. Slough, New Mexico Territory's chief justice. Rynerson pleaded self-defense and was acquitted. Perhaps in the judgment of the day, those circumstances made him eminently qualified to prosecute a murder suspect.

On Hulmes's defense team was Albert J. Fountain, a popular and courageous lawyer. He believed in fairness and justice and owned no allegiance to the power brokers of the day. Seven years later, Mr. Fountain paid for his independence. The mysterious murder of Fountain and his son on their way home from obtaining warrants against some of the region's powerful cattle barons remains unsolved, even though several outlaws (including Sam Ketchum) confessed to the crime.

The public feasted on the Ada Hulmes murder trial. Newspapers catered to this interest by playing up Hulmes's physical attributes and her wicked behavior. The local paper described Hulmes as a "good looking, well-developed young woman of 30 years, with a bright and intelligent countenance and (who) possessed a very nervous temperament." That description was enough to pack the courtroom.

There was no doubt that Hulmes had shot and killed Jack, but the defense argued a claim of self-defense along with a case of insanity. William King, who witnessed the shooting, testified that Brown, who was left-handed, threw his hand against his hip as if he were going for a pistol. King insisted he could see the white handle of a revolver.

The prosecution argued that the bullet had gone through Brown's coat at the point where the revolver was supposed to be. Therefore, his coat would have been closed at the time, preventing the witness from seeing any pistol.

Under oath Hulmes claimed that she had no knowledge of anything that happened from the time she received Jack's note until she found herself in jail. In her defense Dr. W. T. Baird of El Paso testified that Hulmes suffered from a uterine disease known as paralysis of the neck of the bladder and therefore was under nervous strain and tension. He explained she suffered a "loss of accountability." However, local doctor E. L. Stephens wasn't sure if Hulmes's physical condition could be legally defined as insanity.

The defense closed its argument with the facts of Hulmes's childhood in California, where she lived with a caring family and a bright brother. The defense depicted her as a kind, loving daughter who in her teens suffered an overwhelming emotional blow when she lost both her father and brother. These losses, according to the defense, caused her to become distraught and deranged from grief.

In reality Hulmes had been forced to marry young and gave birth to a child at an early age. Her marriage was a nightmare. Her husband spent his days and nights in "riotous living." He abused Hulmes and after squandering her estate, deserted her, leaving her and her child penniless and homeless. Hulmes placed her child in a convent. To support herself and pay for the child's tuition, she took a job as a piano player in a saloon.

The defense went on to describe Brown, the man Hulmes killed, as a desperado and coward. "Gentlemen of the jury, the country loses little when it loses such a man," argued Fielder. He continued his closing argument by reminding the jury that Hulmes's "poor brain was like a seething volcano; it was like an open powder house; it was then, ah, it was then, gentlemen, that Jack Brown purposely, wickedly, lit the fatal fuse." On that passionate note, the defense rested its case.

Prosecutor Rynerson, in his argument, reminded the jury that the county was known for freeing criminals and that he expected this jury to "wipe that slander out of existence and preserve the fair name of Dona Ana County."

District Attorney Wade finished the prosecution's closing statements by summarizing the case and reminding the jury of the severity of Hulmes's crime, which he described as "a dastardly and unprovoked murder." The jury then left to deliberate Hulmes's fate.

All of the jury members believed that Hulmes was guilty, but they disagreed on the penalty she should receive. A few voted in favor of hanging; others wanted her incarcerated, some for fifteen years, some for ten years, and one for three years. Tenaciously that one individual fought for the lesser penalty.

His arguments eventually swung the jury in Hulmes's favor, and at eight o'clock that evening, they returned a verdict of guilty with the recommendation for a three-year sentence in the New Mexico Territorial Penitentiary.

Hulmes had remained stoic and composed throughout the trial, but when the verdict was pronounced, she became hysterical. She was taken from the courtroom to the Rio Grande Hotel, but her hysteria lead to convulsions, and it took two hours for a doctor to revive her.

On the morning of October 30, 1889, Sheriff Harvey Whitehall escorted Hulmes to breakfast at the Exchange Hotel. From there they traveled to the Santa Fe penitentiary by carriage.

As Hulmes left the hotel, a bystander remarked that "a glimpse of the woman as she stepped into the carriage at the hotel revealed a prepossessing face; brown hair and blue eyes over which fell the shade of a jaunty black hat." A reporter at the scene noted that "she wore a black silk dress and a fifty inch seal coat which set off her plump figure in the nobbiest style." It seems the news of the day was a fashion flash on Ada Hulmes.

Hulmes, now prisoner No. 324, was confined to the women's cell on the third floor of the prison. From a heavily grated window, Hulmes could catch a small, distant view of the city of Santa Fe. That fourteen-by-fourteen room was scheduled to be her home for the next three years.

Like most prison systems in the West, the system in New Mexico Territory was not well equipped to handle women prisoners. The room Hulmes occupied was the total prison space for all incarcerated females. She did receive some special treatment; Mrs. H. F. Swope, the wife of the captain of the guard, was assigned as Hulmes's personal matron to attend to whatever prison needs she had.

Hulmes may have been out of sight, but the press saw to it that she was not out of mind. The *Albuquerque Daily Citizen* proclaimed that Hulmes had "more comforts and privileges than any other convict in the land." Her cell was described by the paper as a large, airy third-floor apartment, separate from the main building and with an outstanding view of the Santa Fe valley. The *Citizen* claimed that Hulmes's apartment had carpeted floors and was furnished with a piano. The paper went on to compare Hulmes's treatment with the harsh treatment given a boy who was convicted for stealing a calf, and it ridiculed the $60 a month the state paid for a matron to care for Hulmes.

Not to be outdone by the *Citizen*, the editor of the *Enterprise* criticized the $60 salary as being used "to attend to the every want of this *nymph du pave*." "Pink" Leonard, the editor of the paper, went on to suggest that the penitentiary should be closed and New Mexico prisoners sent to eastern states for "one half the cost to the tax payers."

In early December the New Mexico Board of Prison Commissioners responded to the charges in the newspapers. They stated that the matron was not paid $60 per month, but only $30. They further claimed that the territory did not pay for the piano. As to the supposedly luxurious cell, the board clarified, it "has been the place of confinement of female prisoners since the establishment of the prison, and was constructed for this purpose."

Six months later, the *Las Vegas Optic* uncovered another scandalous story. Sam Griffin, a petty thief from Silver City, told the paper that Hulmes was sharing sexual favors with two employees while her matron was busy attending to the dying warden. At the time Hulmes was believed to still be the prison's only female inmate.

Russell Kistler, the editor of the *Optic*, wanted to be sure of the facts, and he decided to investigate the story. He sent a reporter for an interview with the new warden of the prison, Colonel Edward W. Wynkoop.

Colonel Wynkoop was a tenacious and honorable investigator. Wynkoop stated that he knew nothing of Hulmes's situation before he became warden, but he did clear the record of some fictitious facts. He revealed that Hulmes was not the only woman imprisoned in the Santa Fe facility. For six months Hulmes had shared her cell with Lola Garcia and Baebarita Word, who had been jailed for arson convictions.

A new matron had been appointed to replace Mrs. Swope, who had been instructed by the prison officials to care for her dying husband rather than to her charges. Mrs. Clark, the new matron, testified in court that she had heard stories about some wrongdoings but could not say if there was any truth to the allegations.

Kistler felt that the investigation proved Griffin's claim about Hulmes's behavior in prison, and he printed the story. Other newspapers immediately picked up the scandalous piece and spread it throughout the territory. But other news eventually overshadowed Hulmes's story, and the public forgot her.

At the end of the first year of her sentence, Hulmes lobbied Governor Bradford Prince for an early release. On December 27, the governor received five pages of signatures from Deming, Silver City, and Hermosa, all in support of Hulmes's release. Both Solicitor General Edward Bartlett and Sheriff Whitehall of Grant County signed the petition.

Hulmes initiated a letter-writing campaign to the governor, asking him to visit her. Making a passionate case, she wrote, "Oh, if you had seen me when I first came here and to see me now I don't believe you'd hardly know me." She claimed the recent allegations were politically motivated and were not based in truth. She denied she had been familiar with anyone at the prison. Not above political maneuvering, she declared that her pardon would aid the Republican Party in the forthcoming election. She also wrote that her "nervous system was nearly shattered."

Denver attorney Edgar Caypless entered the fray on Hulmes's side. He described Hulmes as "an artist who had known only the brighter and more beautiful side of life, and whose personal worth was minimally conceded throughout the profession she called her own." Mary Teats, the national superintendent for prison and jail work of the Woman's Christian Temperance Union, disagreed. She described Hulmes as "a dangerous person . . . a contamination . . . who wished to go back to her former wicked life."

In mid-March, Hulmes again wrote Governor Prince about her head troubles and her nervousness. She needed a pardon by June 24 so she could seek work in the theater to support her child and ensure her child's future.

Hulmes also sent a letter to Solicitor General Bartlett reminding him of his promise to help her in obtaining her release. In May Bartlett wrote the governor, insisting that Hulmes should never have been sentenced and noting that since her imprisonment, the public and press had abused her.

The penitentiary physician, Robert H. Longwell, further supported the argument for Hulmes's release. He wrote the governor that "this woman is a nymphomaniac, and to such an extent does she practice this vile habit, that she has developed a suicidal mania. If she is not released from the Penitentiary by Executive clemency she will soon be a raving maniac with no hope of ultimate recovery." Two outside doctors were consulted and both concurred with the diagnosis. One of them, Dr. J. H. Sloan, warned that "we have enough insane people in our Territory without deliberately making another."

In late June the penitentiary superintendent wrote to the governor that Hulmes was rapidly failing and suffering from frequent attacks of mania with suicidal tendencies. On June 29, 1891, after having served less than two years of a three-year sentence, Hulmes was granted a full pardon by the governor and returned to her husband.

The territory may have been finished with Ada Hulmes, but the press was not. The *Santa Fe Sun* ran a story on the night of her release. The paper reported that Sheehan, a man who claimed to be her husband, met her. Sheehan proceeded to get drunk and pass out while Hulmes danced the night away with a twice-convicted horse rustler by the name of Alcario Dominguez. They "made a night of the dance halls and brothels of Santa Fe," the *Sun* wrote.

The *Optic* added a final condemnation, writing: "The career of this woman, and the connection of some of the territorial officials therewith, is one of the most remarkable and shameful pages in all the history of New Mexico. It is doubtful its equal can be found in the civilized world."

After Hulmes's pardon and her riotous evening with Alcario and her supposed husband, she left the territory of New Mexico, and nothing more was heard about her for almost a year. Then on April 8, 1892, the Silver City newspaper reported that Ada Hulmes (which they spelled Humes) was now performing as a variety actress in Creede, Colorado. That was the last time there was any news on Ada Hulmes.

The in-depth reports on Hulmes's crime, trial, incarceration, and pardon leave some questions unanswered. Hulmes's skills as an actress had been highly praised by many in Silver City and other towns. So just how talented was she? Was she skillful enough to play the very believable role of a crazed woman—a role so convincing that two doctors and various law enforcement officers swore it to be true? Or was Hulmes truly an unbalanced woman, a victim of the times, who was persecuted by the public and the press? We know that Hulmes shot Brown; but just how guilty she was remains a mystery.

Vincent Silva

The Man Who Fooled a Town

On October 23, 1892, the residents of Las Vegas, New Mexico, woke up to a picture-perfect winter scene. The previous night's storm had covered the streets and walkways in brilliant white. Shop fronts gleamed with a just-scrubbed look from the night's fierce wind. Windowsills laden with snow glittered and gleamed.

The brilliant sun, reflecting off the icy streets, caused early risers to view the main street with squinted eyes. Then eyes fell on the town bridge. There, gently swaying back and forth in the slight breeze, was Patricio Maes, hanging from the metal girder on the bridge. His clothes, stiff from cold and ice, fit him like boards; his cocked head faced heavenward, as if he were viewing the sky; his sightless eyes saw nothing.

The night before, a bitter wind had swept along the streets of Las Vegas, bringing with it a cold that settled into the marrow of a man's bones. This weather had driven an unusually large crowd to seek comfort in Silva's Imperial Saloon. The conversations thundered off the walls. Red-bearded Vincent Silva, looking dapper and handsome as usual, oiled his way around his customers, stopping here and there to have a quiet word with someone.

Meanwhile, the wind quieted and snow began falling. The white flakes piled up quickly and covered the dusty roads of Las Vegas. As midnight approached, Valdez, the bartender, shouted out that he was feeling sick and was closing the bar. Complaints and surprised looks were exchanged among the men. Silva's never closed; it was a twenty-four-hour-a-day operation. Reluctantly, the men left the saloon, faced with the choice of going home or freezing outside in the cold.

Vicente Silva, crime lord extraordinaire

Courtesy Palace of the Governors (MNM/DCA), #143691

When the bar emptied, Silva locked the door and started for home. However, a short time later, shadowy figures began making their way through the snow to the saloon's side door. Vincent Silva had called an emergency meeting of his secret outlaw band, the White Caps. Silva, a respected and wealthy citizen of Las Vegas, was not all he appeared to be.

Silva's handsome looks, powerful bearing, and red hair made him a charismatic man. Most of the townspeople held him in high regard as a successful businessman and the owner of the Imperial Saloon, a large affair with a bar, billiards, and a dance hall.

Silva came to Las Vegas with his wife, Telesfora, in 1875 and started his business. Four years later the Atchison, Topeka, and Santa Fe Railway arrived, making his saloon even more successful.

Wealth and success were something new to Silva. He was born of poor parents in the countryside of Bernallilo County, New Mexico. He married Telesfora Sandoval, a plain-looking village girl who presented a remarkable contrast to his handsome looks.

Before moving to Las Vegas, Silva and Telesfora lived in the mining town of San Pedro. Silva operated a grocery store, and his wife took care of the candy counter. An avid hunter, Silva spent his weekends looking for game. His familiarity with the countryside served him well in later years.

In Las Vegas people admired Silva as a family man. He was the doting father of an adopted daughter. Eight years earlier, someone had abandoned the newborn Emma in a Las Vegas stable. Unable to bear children, Telesfora begged her husband to adopt the baby. It was not long before both parents were completely enamored with the child. As further evidence of his family responsibilities, Silva had welcomed Telesflora's younger brother, Gabriel, into his household and employed him as a bartender in his saloon.

Silva was more than a family man, however. He had another side—a dark, evil side that only his outlaw band knew. His greed had slowly turned a simple man into a crime lord. While he smiled and sympathized with the citizens of Las Vegas, his men were rustling cattle, robbing, and murdering innocent people.

Vincent had built an organization with some of the cruelest, most immoral men in the West; men with no conscience and no compassion. Some of his gang members bore very descriptive names. They called Martin Gonzoles y Blea "the Moor" because of his dark complexion; Manuel Gonzales y Baca, "Toothless"; Antonio Jose Valdez, "the Ape"; and Ricardo Romero, "Pugnose." Antonio Jose Valdez earned the name "Pussyfoot" for the way he walked.

Not all of the outlaws were tagged by their physical appearance. Guadalupe Catallero, "the Owl," was Silva's spy and personal aide. Five feet tall and weighing about one hundred and ten pounds with crossed eyes, the Owl had the appearance of a helpless and harmless man.

The Owl looked so inconsequential; people often ignored him. He would sit on his haunches on the side of the street or by a storefront and appear to be slumbering. However, he was wide awake; he would listen, take everything in, and then report his findings to Silva.

Also in the gang were three men of extreme importance to Vincent: Julian Trujillo, Jose Chavez y Chavez, and Eugenio Alarid. These three were members of the Las Vegas police force. They had worked over the years to see to it that Vincent Silva was not accused or even suspected of crimes.

Vincent Silva was an uneducated man; he could barely read and write, but his cunning, ambition, and ruthless manner made him the leader of this group. His men followed him without question.

To keep his façade of respectability in the community, Vincent had to keep his unlawful acts away from public scrutiny. He bought a ranch, Monte Largo, in an inaccessible section of the San Pedro mining district. Monte Largo was a place of deep gorges and scissor peaks, an ideal hiding place for his rustled cattle and horses.

It was to Monte Largo that Refugio Esquivel, a local rancher, traced his stolen horses. There he found his brand altered into Silva's brand.

After rescuing his stock, Refugio stormed into Silva's saloon and accused him of cattle rustling.

Silva feigned innocence. There was no proof, so who would believe Refugio? However, the humiliation of a public accusation in his own saloon shook Silva's confidence. For years missing cattle and unsolved murders had plagued Las Vegas, but no one had ever suspected the respectable Vincent Silva. Someone must have talked. Silva believed that there was an informer in the White Caps, and he thought he knew who it was.

Silva acted the part of a fair man, and the fair thing to do was to have the alleged traitor put on trial and judged by his peers. And so it was on that snowy night in October that the band of thieves gathered on the second floor of the Imperial Saloon for a clandestine meeting.

Just days before, Patricio Maes, a Silva gang member, had placed a notice announcing his resignation from the Partido del Pueblo Unido political party. He stated he was now a member of the Republican Party.

The Herrera brothers, who wanted a party that represented the people, originally started the Partido del Pueblo Unido. These men rode around the countryside punishing those they believed had stolen or illegally obtained land from the poorer peasants. While they threatened people and destroyed barns and crops, they never physically attacked anyone. The party was nicknamed the White Caps after the headgear they wore on raids. When Pablo Herrera was murdered, the party was leaderless and disbanded. Vincent Silva secretly reformed the party into a gang of thieves, murderers, and cattle rustlers. He took on the name the White Caps for his gang. They were also called the Forty Thieves, a name that accurately described the membership.

Silva took the published announcement of Maes's resignation personally. To him it was not a resignation from a political party, but a display of disloyalty and untrustworthiness. He also believed that Maes was the leak.

Silva set up court to try Maes on the charge of being a White Cap traitor. He appointed himself attorney general and fellow outlaw

Polanco the defending lawyer. Toothless, also called The Dull One, was the judge.

Both sides presented their arguments. The gang members voted on a verdict, but "Judge" Toothless felt the verdict was unfair and refused to announce it. In an angry tirade directed at Toothless because of his refusal, Manuel Gonzolez y Baca hurled insults at the men, reminding them of the importance of capital punishment. The discussion heated up as men chose sides and began to make their points physically. It was apparent to Silva that each member of his band had his own opinion about the accused and was not willing to listen to other arguments, or to blindly follow Silva on this matter.

Silva stopped the trial, ordered three gallons of whiskey, and after the refreshing break, called for another vote. The vote was unanimous— death to the traitor. Patricio Maes fell to his knees pleading for mercy, proclaiming his innocence, and begging for forgiveness for any transgressions. But the liquor had done its job, and the gang members were now in agreement with Silva and unmoved by Maes's pleading.

A noose dropped over Maes's head, and the gang led their victim through the deserted, stormy streets to the iron bridge spanning the Gallinas River. When they reached the bridge, the assassins allowed Maes to say his prayers. When he finished, one end of the rope was tied to a girder. Then Silva and a gang member picked up Maes and threw him over the bridge. Unfortunately, the rope knot was not tight, and it slipped, causing Maes to fall, smashing against the ice of the frozen river.

Two men climbed down to the ice, threw the loose end up, and the men on the bridge hauled Maes's body up. They tightly secured the rope end to the metal bridge girder and let him hang. Then, in ones and twos, the gang members drifted off, leaving Maes to his death dance in the howling wind. The next morning a large crowd gathered around the bridge to view the swinging corpse of Patricio Maes.

The *Las Vegas Optic* reported the hanging with a small notice: "Patricio Maes was taken by a mob early Saturday morning and hanged from the Gallinas River bridge at Las Vegas." That seemed to be the end of the matter.

Meanwhile, Captain Esquivel, the father of Refugio, was quietly investigating the rustling of his family's horses. Captain Esquivel had enough evidence to prove the illegal activities of the White Caps. Unfortunately, it was all circumstantial. Even so, he was able to get a grand jury indictment against Silva. On November 7, 1892, Vincent Silva's trial began. At the trial Silva's alibi could not be broken. The charges were dropped, and Silva was freed.

After that Silva became a very cautious man. He did not fear the local police, but the Sociedad de Muta Protection, a vigilante group. Taking several gang members with him, Silva went into hiding in a cave near the village of Coyote (now called Rainsville). From this hideout, a mere twelve miles from Las Vegas, Silva and his band continued their criminal activities.

A deserted Telesfora was forced to find a way to support herself and Emma, by now a student at the Las Vegas Academy. She opened a lunch counter in town and then, fearing for the safety of her brother, Gabriel, insisted that he give up his work at the saloon, which continued operating under the management of a gang member. Although he was no longer managing the saloon, Silva did not stay completely away from the town. He made clandestine night forays into West Las Vegas to visit his mistress, Flora de la Pena.

Silva knew his safety depended on stealth and secrecy, and he worried about the two people closest to him. His young brother-in-law, Gabriel Sandoval, knew too much about Silva's illegal activities. His other worry was for the safety of Telesfora and his child.

Telesfora was the opposite of Silva in many ways. Her short, dark, and fat appearance made a sharp contrast to his large frame and red-headed good looks. Despite her unattractiveness she was well respected in the community and known as a kind and compassionate woman. Her demeanor was quiet; Silva's was one of boldness and bravado. She was blindly dedicated to Silva and very much in love with him; he openly kept a mistress. What the two had in common was their love for their daughter, Emma. Now Silva was to use that love to protect himself.

On January 23, Guadalupe Catallero pulled up to the Las Vegas Academy in a horse-drawn carriage. He told Emma he was taking her home for lunch. Instead, he drove her to Silva, who took her to Taos and enrolled her in a local school.

When Telesfora found her daughter missing, she was frantic, consumed with worry and fear for her beloved child. By kidnapping Emma, Silva hoped to silence both his brother-in-law and his wife. He planned on using Telesfora and her brother's love for Emma and their fear for her well-being to force them into cooperating with him. But Silva soon worried that even this measure was not enough. Enlisting the help of his three police officers, Jose Chavez y Chavez, Julian Trujillo, and Eugenio Alarid, he planned a murder.

The three policemen met with Gabriel Sandoval. Convincing him that he was aiding in the rescue of Emma, they led him to an abandoned mill in West Las Vegas. There Silva jumped out of the darkness and stabbed Sandoval, his own brother-in-law, to death, while the three police officers held his arms. The policemen, with the help of the Owl, carried the body to the back of Silva's saloon, where they stripped it and threw it the privy pit.

Silva had plans to leave for Mexico with his mistress, but he needed more money. Silva and five of his gang members broke into the William Frank mercantile store in Las Vegas and helped themselves. They also stole the safe. The *Las Vegas Optic* described it as "the most audacious act in many years."

The thieves dumped the broken safe by the road about a mile from the store, setting fire to the accounts, books, and papers. They took the cash, amounting to twenty-five dollars. The merchandise, which was worth more than $500, was never recovered.

On May 19, 1893, a notice of a reward for the capture of the outlaws appeared in the *Las Vegas Optic*. On the list was Vincent Silva, wanted for two indictments for stealing. Also on the list were rewards for the capture of the robbers of the William Frank Store and the murderers of Jacob Stutzman and Abran Abulafie, all by persons unknown. What the authorities did not know at the time was that all of these crimes were perpetrated by Silva and his band of forty thieves.

On the day this notice appeared, events took a horrific turn in Vincent Silva's life. Needing more money for his flight with his mistress, Silva sent his wife a message. The message told Telesfora that he, her brother, and Emma were all well and that she was to pack her things and join them.

That evening, Silva's man Genovevo Avila picked Telesfora up and headed toward Silva's ranch. Along the way, Vincent joined them. When they reached the ranch, Silva dragged his wife into the small house and demanded money. She handed him all she had—$200. Not satisfied, Silva demanded her jewelry. When she protested, he pulled out his knife and killed her. He dragged her body to a deep arroyo at the southern end of the village and flung her to the bottom.

Furious, Silva jumped on the bank until it collapsed and covered her body. After he'd killed his wife, his mood drastically changed. Pleased with himself, he opened up his stuffed money belt, and gave each of his five gang members $10.

The men were in a state of shock over the killing of Telesfora. But shock turned to anger when Silva handed out the meager sum of $10 each from his bulging money belt.

As the men headed for the village, Antonio Jose Valdez walked up to Silva, put a .45 to his head, and shot him. They dragged his body back to the bank of the arroyo, tossed it over, kicked sand down to cover it, and went their separate ways after dividing up the money and jewels.

The fact that Vincent Silva, Telesfora Silva, and Gabriel Sandoval were all now dead did not slow down the activities of the White Caps. Over the next few years, innocent men were murdered, and cattle continued to disappear. Finally, William T. Thornton, the governor of New

Mexico, offered pardons to anyone who came forward with information on the crimes.

It was not until April 10, 1894, that Manuel Gonzoles y Baca told the district attorney about the crimes of Vincent Silva and the White Caps. Among the many crimes he reported was the hanging of Patricio Maes and the murder of Gabriel Sandoval. He said nothing of the murder of Telesfora and Vincent Silva.

When the news of Vincent's heinous crimes became public, the townsfolk were appalled. A man they had respected, trusted, and admired had betrayed them. An intense hunt for Silva turned up nothing. Vincent Silva and his wife seemed to have disappeared without a trace.

Vincent's mistress, Flor de la Pena, took Emma into her home and raised her along with her son, Hilario, who may have been Silva's child.

Eventually, the Silva gang began to fall apart. Several gang members had been captured and hanged. Dishonest policemen Julian Trujillo and Eugenio Alarid had earned life sentences in prison. Jose Chavez y Chavez escaped and went into hiding. And Vincent Silva was still "missing."

A year later, Guadalupe Caballero, the Owl, solved the mystery of Vincent and Telesfora Silva's whereabouts and explained to the authorities how they had been killed. On March 17, 1895, Antonio Jose Valdez led the officials to their graves in the arroyo. The March 18 edition of the *Las Vegas Optic* reported the events:

> Some excitement was caused here yesterday by the bringing in of the bodies of Vincent Silva and his wife. Silva was the leader of the gang of cut throats who made so much trouble in this county two years ago. He has been badly wanted by the officers since the gang was broken up, and there were rumors that he had been killed and also that he was in Arizona or Colorado. Yesterday Hon. Manuel Baca and a party went out about 12 miles north of here on information obtained from some of the former gang, and found the bodies of both

Silva and wife buried near each other. It is understood that Silva was murdered to obtain money supposed to be in his possession and his wife was killed to keep her from informing on the murderers.

Finally, after two years of searching, the authorities found Vincent Silva, a man who led two lives. It was a shock to the town to discover that the man they respected as a successful businessman, loving husband, and devoted father was a killer, thief, adulterer, and kidnapper. With his cleverness and wit, Silva had managed to fool a town for more than twenty years.

Thomas Edward "Black Jack" Ketchum and His Gang
The Man Who Lost His Head

On January 30, 1896, a cold January wind furiously attacked the Lincoln County courthouse, but nothing could chill Colonel Albert J. Fountain's exuberance. He almost skipped down the steps as he left the courthouse. In his pocket he had what he came for—thirty-two indictments for men who had been stealing cattle and altering brands. Some of New Mexico's most important ranchers were named in those indictments.

Colonel Fountain was the special investigator and prosecutor for the Southeastern New Mexico Stock Growers Association. For years the suspects named in the indictment had robbed the honest ranchers and gone unpunished. At last there would be justice.

The colonel's eight-year-old son, Henry, scampered after his father. He was secretly glad this boring visit was over and they were heading back home to Mesilla. He accompanied his father only because his mother believed his presence would protect his father from harm. With typical youthful imagination, he visualized himself as a hero fighting off the bad men who would dare to attack his father. But other than falling down the steps in his haste, Henry didn't see much danger around.

A cowboy emerged from the crowd around the courthouse and shoved a note into Fountain's hands. Henry peeked over his father's arm as he read the note: "If you drop this we will be your friends. If you go on with it, you will never reach home alive."

Henry, wide-eyed with fear, looked at his father, who gave a snort of a laugh and crumpled the note. Nothing was going to ruin the colonel's

Sent to hell without his head, Thomas "Black Jack" Ketchum is shown before his execution in Clayton, New Mexico.

Arizona Historical Society/Tucson, AHS #12720

good mood, not cowardly threats, not a slow-moving justice system. The note only managed to inflame his bravado.

Henry and his father started for home. It was going to be a long drive in the buggy, and the colonel planned to spend two nights along the way with friends.

On February 1, Henry and the colonel left Dave Sutherland's home for the final leg of their trip home, a seventy-mile route along a lonely road. The road would take them around White Sands, through the San Agustin Pass, down to Las Cruces, and on to Mesilla. About halfway into the trip the colonel and his son crossed paths with Saturnino Barela. Saturnino was on his mail run to Tularosa. The two men stopped their horses and chatted.

Barela noticed the rifle resting across Colonel Fountain's knees. When he asked the colonel about the gun, Fountain pointed toward the ridge that ran parallel to the road. "See those three riders? They've been following me since I left town. Recognize them?"

Barela took a long, hard look, but the riders were far away and rode with their hats pulled low. "Can't say that I do, Colonel, but you be careful."

The next day on the return ride, Barela stopped at a spot a short distance from where he and the colonel had talked. He spotted buckboard tracks heading off the road. These tracks were soon joined by the tracks of horsemen. Arriving in Las Cruces, Barela inquired about the colonel, only to be told he had never arrived home.

With a sense of urgency, the men in town formed a posse to search for the missing father and son. At Chalk Hill, where the buckboard left the road, the riders spotted dried bloodstains on the ground and a bloodstained handkerchief. The posse followed the tracks, which eventually led them to the colonel's abandoned carriage, but there were no signs of the horses, Fountain's rifle, his blankets, or the pinto pony he was bringing home.

The ground around the carriage was littered with legal papers. One of the riders pointed out a necktie knotted on one of the buggy's wheels.

The trail continued. The posse followed the horse tracks for several more miles, only to lose the trail when the tracks merged with cattle hoofprints.

The disappearance of the colonel and his son remained a mystery until 1899 when Sam Ketchum, brother of Tom "Black Jack" Ketchum, attemped to solved the mystery on his deathbed. Incarcerated in the Santa Fe Prison, dying from blood poisoning, Sam felt the need to confess to Bob Lewis, the Socorro County deputy.

Sam knew he was about to meet his maker, and the horrible secret he had carried for years was too much for the dying man. "Tom killed that Colonel Fountain and his son. Someone else rode with us, but I ain't telling you who that was." Sam paused, and the guilt he felt was evident in his confession. "I pleaded with Tom, begged him, not to kill the kid, but Tom said we couldn't have any witnesses."

Apparently Sam Ketchum had a conscience. Not so, his brother Tom, who was never known for a kind act or a kind word.

Thomas Edward Ketchum was born on October 31, 1863, in Richland Creek, San Saba County, Texas. Tom was the youngest child of five. His brother Barry was twelve years older, and Sam was five. Tom also had two older sisters.

When Tom was five years old, his father, Green Berry Ketchum, died. Five years later, his mother, Temperance Katherine Wydick Ketchum, died. Tom's mother had been blind and unable to offer much in the way of an upbringing for her children before her death. The older siblings, who were little more than teenagers, raised Tom. Both Sam and Tom were tall, strong teenagers who earned their keep working on neighboring cattle ranches. Of the Ketchum brothers, Tom was the most dangerous, and even as a youth his behavior was erratic. He had a bad temper and was hard to get along with.

It was another outlaw who inspired Tom's sobriquet. William "Black Jack" Christianson and his gang had terrorized Arizona and New Mexico with a number of robberies and murders. Christianson was tracked and shot by a posse in Clifton, Arizona, on March 29, 1897. His reputation, and his nickname, appealed to Tom Ketchum, who from that time on chose to be called Black Jack Ketchum. That was the name he lived by, and that was the name he died by.

Unlike Tom, Sam was considered to be a sensible young man during his younger years. However, when his wife left him and took their two children, it broke him. He turned to his brother and started an outlaw life.

It seems that a woman was the cause for both brothers turning to lawless ways. Tom was rejected by a woman he wanted to make his wife, and the rejection was more than this sullen man could handle. He met Cora when he was working as a cowboy. Tom pledged her his true love and told her they would marry when he returned from the cattle drive. The parting was passionate and public. When Tom reached an overnight cattle stop, a messenger delivered a letter from Cora. His elation was quickly dampened when he read her heartless words.

> You remember the day I told you farewell and wept a little and told you I could never love another. That was a little bait fixed up especially for your benefit. C. G. Slim was standing nearby looking on and you'd no more than got out of sight when we went down to Staton and got married. Signed Mrs. Cora Slim.

Tom read the letter to the other cowboys then whipped out his six-shooter and beat himself in the head. He continued until he staggered into the creek, standing in water up to his boot tops, then took his lariat and pelted his body. There was no doubt that Tom was an unstable man, and a dangerous one. Any good, any compassion that Tom had in him died that day.

His behavior cannot be totally blamed on his "Dear John" letter; however, he had never been a model citizen. From his youth his misdeeds were numerous. He was accused of stealing horses, was arrested for disturbing the peace, and was a suspect in an unsuccessful robbery at the ranch of a woman who was seven and a half months pregnant.

Although the robbery was not successful, Tom and his cohorts managed to set fire to the ranch house. Fortunately, the quick-thinking woman saved herself and two children.

On December 12, 1895, Tom's career took a serious and dangerous turn. He and some pals were accused of ambushing and killing John N. "Jap" Powers near his farm in Knickerbocker, Texas. There was talk that Powers's wife instigated the killing.

A grand jury issued warrants for the arrest of Tom Ketchum, Dave Atkins, and Bud Upshaw. Typical of the times, the warrants were never served because the trio disappeared.

A few months later Sam, who was operating a saloon and crooked gambling hall in Texas, was forced to shut down his business. He joined his brother, Tom, who was now in New Mexico Territory.

Going by the aliases Welch and Steve, Tom and Sam showed up at the Bell Ranch looking for work. Usually cowboys welcomed new hands, but the old hands on the Bell were intuitively suspicious of these two.

Late in the evening of June 8, 1896, the brothers broke into the ranch storeroom, stole some supplies, and rode out. Tom Kane, wagon boss and part-time deputy, saw them leave. He trailed them to Fort Sumner. There he learned the two had acquired fresh horses at the nearby Chevez Ranch. Kane's posse picked up the Ketchums' trail and followed it down the Pecos River. There they lost it when it joined tracks left by a herd of cattle. (One of the strategies of outlaws on the run was to find a fresh cattle track and mingle their tracks with those of the cattle in the churned-up earth.)

But the stolen Bell Ranch supplies were not enough to keep the Ketchums going. On June 10, they rode into Liberty, New Mexico, thirty miles from the Bell Ranch.

Just before daybreak Tom spotted the small store and post office owned by Morris and Levi Herzstein. It was a perfect setup for him. Tom and Sam broke in, took what they needed in supplies, including blankets and clothing, and pocketed $250 in cash. Then they rode out, heading southwest with their loot.

Later that day the Herzstein brothers discovered the break-in. Twenty-two-year-old Levi Herzstein wasn't going to let anyone get away with robbing his store. He rounded up Merejildo Gallegos, Placido Gurule, and Atancio Borque. The four headed out, tracking the robbers.

Tom and Sam were stopped for a meal when they spotted four riders bearing down on them; the Ketchums grabbed their rifles and opened fire. Herzstein, Gallegos, and Gurule went down in the first few volleys. But Black Jack Ketchum wasn't satisfied. He approached the downed men and emptied his rifle into the bodies of Herzstein and Gallegos. Several of the horses were killed in the fight, but Borque was able to escape on foot.

Borque had traveled only a short distance when he met Sam Goldsmith and Harry Edwards. The three of them returned to the bloody scene of the murders. To their surprise they found that Gurule was alive and had suffered only a flesh wound. He had saved his life by pretending to be dead. But Herzstein and Gallegos were not so lucky—their bodies were a testimony to Black Jack Ketchum's wrath. For years there was no proof that the Ketchums were the two responsible for this robbery and murder. Then, four years later, Placido Gurule spotted Tom Ketchum at the Las Vegas, New Mexico, train station. Tom was being escorted to a court appearance. "That's him," Gurule yelled. Then he proceeded to identify Ketchum as one of the two men who killed Herzstein and Gallegos. However, again there were no formal charges made. No reason was ever given for this oversight. Sometimes the law was lax on the western frontier. And Las Vegas was known to have lawmen of questionable honesty.

After the Liberty robbery and subsequent murder of Herzstein and Gallegos, Black Jack laid low. Several other unsavory characters joined Tom and Sam, and the Black Jack Gang was formed.

No one could accuse Black Jack Ketchum of having a sense of humor or a pleasing personality. He was sullen, quiet, and unfriendly. As for the sense of humor, well, the best example is when some dinner companions played a practical joke on him. It began when they kept passing the butter between themselves, keeping it out of Black Jack's reach.

When Black Jack had had enough, he drew out his gun, pointed it at the strangers, and commanded that they eat all the butter on the table. When they were done with what was on the table, Black Jack ordered a couple more pounds brought in from the kitchen, and then told the strangers to finish that since they seemed "so fond of the stuff."

After a while the Black Jack Gang turned its attention to bigger stakes—train robberies. On May 14, 1897, they stopped a Southern Pacific train in southwest Texas near the Mexican border, entered the locomotive cab, and made the engineer halt the train. Successfully forcing their way into the express car, they placed dynamite on top of the safe, placed a side of beef on top of that, and blew the whole thing up. They got away with $42,000.

After the robbery the gang headed for Cimarron, New Mexico Territory, and holed up at the luxurious St. James Hotel. There they lived an extravagant life, throwing money around the gaming tables and saloon.

When they had had enough of the good life or maybe when they ran out of money, they decided to get back to business. And their first order of business was to establish a hideout in Turkey Canyon, ten miles southwest of Cimarron.

The gang built three wooden shacks in a flat area surrounded by trees, well hidden in the hills around Cimarron. Having what they considered a safe hideaway, the gang planned its next move.

On September 3, 1897, they hit the Colorado and Southern passenger train outside of Folsom, New Mexico Territory. It is estimated they got between $14,000 and $15,000.

Over the next two years, the Black Jack Gang was suspected of robbing more than seven trains. Not all of their attempts were successful, but they had enough success to be considered notorious train robbers.

But time was running out for the Black Jack Gang, and what proved to be their undoing was a comedy of errors.

The gang returned to its Turkey Canyon hideout to plan its next robbery. They decided to repeat an earlier success. On July 11, 1899, Sam and two other gang members hit the Colorado and Southern again, at almost the exact spot where they had previously robbed the train. For some reason Black Jack was not with them. Sam and the boys collected between $20,000 and $70,000 in payroll money. They left not only an empty safe but also an angry conductor bent on retribution and revenge.

In Walsenburg, Colorado, Sheriff Edward Farr got news of the Colorado and Southern robbery. The robbery was too close to his territory, so he headed out to do some outlaw hunting. In New Mexico he picked up U.S. Marshal Forsaker and a posse made up of Perfecto Cordova, H. M. Love, Little Reno, a newcomer to the West called F. H. Smith, and J. H. Morgan. Morgan was familiar with the Black Jack Gang's whereabouts and suggested they look in Turkey Canyon.

It was purely a stroke of luck that the posse found the hideout. In the ensuing battle Sam Ketchum was wounded. Sheriff Farr was hit in the chest, the bullet driving downward so forcefully that it killed him instantly and splashed his blood over Smith, whose desire for adventure was answered with a dose of western reality.

Three days after the shootout, a posse found the wounded Sam Ketchum and brought him into Cimarron on a stretcher. A few days later, on July 24, he died in the Santa Fe prison, but not before making his confession regarding the deaths of Colonel Fountain and his son.

It is doubtful that Black Jack Ketchum knew his gang had hit the Colorado and Southern train or that his brother had died. For if he did, he then committed an incredible act of stupidity. Acting alone, he robbed the same train on August 16, at the exact spot the train had been hit twice before by the Black Jack Gang.

This time Conductor Frank Harrington was waiting for him. As Black Jack approached the express car, Harrington unloaded his twelve-gauge, taking off most of Black Jack's right arm between the elbow and shoulder. Black Jack escaped in the darkness, but the next day train crews picked up a badly wounded man who identified himself as George Stevens. The alias did not save Ketchum from arrest and trial. He was rushed to Santa Fe where the prison doctor amputated his arm. He pulled through only to face a hanging sentence.

In 1887 the Territory of New Mexico passed a bill that assigned the death penalty to anyone who "would willfully assault any train, car, or locomotive with intent to commit robbery, murder, or any other felony upon the engineer, brakeman, conductor, mail or express agent, or passenger." Black Jack was sentenced under that law.

On April 26, 1901, in Clayton, New Mexico Territory, they hanged Black Jack Ketchum. It was with a great deal of bravado that the one-armed man swaggered up to the gallows. As he mounted the steps he announced to his audience, "I'll be in hell before you start breakfast, boys." Black Jack Ketchum, murderer, train robber, and rustler, knew where he was going.

His last request was for music. He stood on the gallows while the sweet strains of guitar and violin played "Just as the Sun Went Down" and "Amelia Waltzes."

It was not an easy execution. It was the first hanging for the town of Clayton, and the inexperienced gallows men made some mistakes. The rope had not been stretched properly, the executioner did not measure Black Jack's height for the depth of the drop, and the wrong weights were put on Black Jack's feet. As the trapdoor sprung backward, Black Jack dropped swiftly. His feet landed hard on the ground beneath the gallows. A dark reddish ring appeared around the hood. When it was removed, Black Jack's head rolled out. He had been decapitated in the hanging.

There were some old-timers who insisted that Black Jack Ketchum was never hanged. He escaped. They claimed that what the hanging crowd saw was a three-day-old corpse on the gallows, which is why the head was severed from the body when the trap sprung. But proof that the man they hanged was alive can be found in the supposed comments expressed by the victim. And a close look at the many pictures of the hanging shows a man very much alive, with one arm, and a noose around his neck. So in death, Black Jack Ketchum, a man who couldn't control his temper or his outlaw ways, lost his head for the last time.

Pancho Villa's
Last Chance for Glory
The Raid on Columbus, March 9, 1916

The men moved noiselessly, surefooted on the desert sand they had called home for generations. There were no shadows in the moonless night. They were men with little education, all with a hunger for a better life. Pancho Villa had gathered these men and boys from small, poor villages, promising them work, money, a white woman for each man, and schooling for the boys. It was dreams of wealth the men followed, not thoughts of power. In the middle of the night, the men made their way in small groups to a point about three miles west of the border gate.

While most held a military rank, they were not a legitimate army. One in twenty was a general, and there were many colonels. Villa handed out ranks as favors, not as positions earned. He believed titles gave an air of legitimacy to his ragtag army of banditos called "Villistas."

Villa himself had humble beginnings. He was born Doroteo Arango Arámbula in Durango, Mexico. An uneducated man, son of a peasant, he killed his first man at sixteen when he discovered the son of a hacienda owner had seduced his sister and then abandoned her. After the killing he stole a horse, headed for the mountains, and began his outlaw life.

During his lifetime he was on both sides of the law. An outlaw, he robbed banks, trains, and stores and committed forgery and murder. He was a revolutionary leader, and at one time held the office of governor of Chihuahua and printed his own money.

Pancho Villa
Photo courtesy of The Silver City Museum Society

However, when he mounted the attack on Columbus, he had lost his legitimacy and political status and was nothing more than an outlaw in charge of a band of thieves.

Pancho Villa placed Colonel Cardenas in charge of this attack. Villa opted to stay back in the mountains and await the news. As the banditos approached Columbus, New Mexico, Cardenas divided his men into two groups. Half stayed with him and were equipped with an 8-mm light machine gun, which he set up on a low hill facing the town. The rest went with Colonel Cervantes to attack the town from its east end. Then the men hunkered down and waited.

Pancho Villa had conceived a brazen plan—a raid on Columbus, New Mexico. This plan was his chance for glory and power. Spies had informed him that a safe stuffed with money was located in Sam Ravel's general store. Pancho had some unfinished business with Ravel. He had placed an order with Ravel and paid him for guns and ammunition. However, Ravel never delivered the merchandise, nor did he give back the money. Pancho was going to take care of that matter. With this raid he would get his money and the supplies he desperately needed. His orders to his men were simple. Surprise the gringos and loot all buildings.

Columbus was a small, dusty town of about five hundred people located just over the Mexican border. It had a thriving business district that included two hotels, a newspaper, a bank, and a post office. It also had Camp Furlough.

The U.S. military set up small army outposts along the border in an attempt to stop the increasing incursion of Mexican bandits and rustlers. Camp Furlough was one of these outposts. It normally had about five hundred men and twenty-one officers, but on this day had fewer. Many of the officers were out of town, including the commanding officer, Colonel Herbert Slocum, who, with his wife, was visiting Deming.

The army camp at Columbus made the plan for a raid even more audacious and appealing to Pancho. However, Villa never counted on the heavy losses he would sustain. Four hundred Villistas started their trek toward Columbus. More than a hundred would never make it home.

Dawn was still hiding behind the mountains when Sergeant Ellery Waters finished checking his five posts and picket lines. That's when the guard, Private Fred Griffin, noticed movement in the darkness. He called for the password, and when silence greeted him, he started shooting.

The early morning peace erupted in gunfire. Then there were shouts of "viva Mexico," "viva Villa," "death to the gringos." The bandits over-ran Griffin, killing him. The charging Villistas shot indiscriminately. A wayward bullet hit the railroad clock, stopping it at 4:30 a.m.

When Sergeant Waters heard the shots, he took off for the orderly room, unlocking it as the Mexican raiders filled the streets. He stood by the door, guarding the rifles within and triggering off twenty-one rounds from his service pistol to keep the bandits at bay.

Sergeant Burns unlocked the rifle case as troopers came running in to grab weapons. The ammunition, however, was in the locked supply room, and no one could find the sergeant who held the key. Turns out he was hiding under the water tank. Burns and Waters broke down the door and rapidly handed out bandoleers of .30-06 cartridges to the scrambling troopers.

Two soldiers were early causalities when bullets pierced their wooden barracks walls, killing them. Corporal Harry Wiswell died near the border gate, and Private Jessie Taylor died from his wounds the next day at the Fort Bliss hospital.

Two of the Villistas had orders to go to Sam Ravel's home and capture Sam and his two brothers. They were to take them to the store, force Sam to open the safe, and then shoot him. But when Ortiz and Vargas arrived at the Ravel house, they found only the youngest brother, Arthur, a boy of fifteen. Louis was hiding under a pile of hides. The men dragged Arthur to the store and ordered him to open the safe. When it became apparent that the younger Ravel did not have the combination, the Mexicans attempted to get into the safe by shooting at the knob. The gunfire caused the gasoline drums in front of an adjacent store to explode, and both stores caught fire.

Meanwhile, Lieutenants John Lucas and J. P. Castleman went for the army's machine guns. They were able to answer the bandits' shots with a steady flow of bullets, and slowly the army's greater firepower began to take its toll on the raiders. Sergeant Harry Dobbs held the line for Lieutenant Castleman and the troopers as they prepared their defense line in front of the Hoover Hotel. Fatally wounded, Sergeant Dobbs stayed in position firing until he died from loss of blood. Sergeant Dobbs was recommended for a Medal of Honor; unfortunately, it was never approved.

A group of Villa's men headed for the hotel to sack the rooms. Here they met Uncle Stephan Birchfield. Awakened from his sleep, an irritated Uncle Stephan told the looters to stop making so much noise. They had him in their gun sights when he presented them with a proposition. If they let him go, he would write checks made out to cash for them. One man in the group had had dealings with Uncle Stephan and knew him to be good for his word. While machine guns and rifles were blazing around him, Uncle Stephan wrote checks and lived.

Mexicans set fire to the wooden-frame Columbus Hotel, but not before they captured the proprietor, William Ritchie. His daughter begged the raiders not to kill her father. Her pleas went unheeded, however. They shot him and burned his body along with the hotel. Juan Favela was able to rescue the rest of the Ritchies. Most of the Columbus Hotel guests fled the fire by running out the back door and through the backyard. John Walker and Dr. H. M. Hart died when they tried to escape out the front door.

When the shooting started, Charles Miller left his hotel room to get rifles from his drugstore. He made it as far as the hotel door. Milton James and his pregnant wife, Bessie, made a run for the Hoover Hotel and its protecting thick adobe walls. They were shot as they reached the door. Will Hoover pulled Bessie into the hotel. Her last words were, "Thank God we are safe."

Alice Bains, a sister of Bessie James, found the hotel office filled with Mexicans. In fear she ran between the buildings and out into the bush and hid until daylight, when she saw the Villistas retreating.

Later, Mrs. Sara Hoover wrote her brother about the shocking events:

> Our soldiers and our citizens never dreamed that Villa would cross the border to murder innocent women and children. They did think he might cross to steal horses and cattle, and our soldiers were scattered along the border. Our people think Villa has had spies here who have kept him informed of the troops along the border, and he could safely cross the line and murder a lot of American citizens, which would bring on war and unite the Mexicans. He must have known that in the end the Mexicans would be defeated, yet he would hold a high place in Mexican affairs . . . there will be no war and Villa will be hunted down as a bandit and murderer and will lose his life.

Young Arthur Ravel saved the life of Sara Hoover's son Will when he convinced the bandits that Will was out of town. Will Hoover was the owner of the Hoover Hotel, the town banker, and its mayor.

As the Villistas headed for the bank, soldiers opened fire. One bandito lay dead in front of the hotel, six others lined the street, and bandito bodies were scattered over the other main streets of Columbus.

As dawn broke over the smoking, devastated town, a broken and beaten bandito band regrouped and retreated. Except for the devastation, they had accomplished none of their objectives. They left about one hundred of their comrades dead and seven as wounded prisoners. Ten American officers and soldiers lost their lives, as did eight civilians. Two officers, five soldiers, and two civilians suffered wounds.

One of the wounded bandits was a young boy of twelve. He pleaded for his life, saying he was told the gringos would kill him if he were captured. Jesus came from a poor village. His job with the banditos was to clean and care for their horses. He told his captors that once, due to

113

exhaustion on a long trail ride, he fell out of his saddle, and the officers beat him and told him to keep going.

The *Deming Headlight* reported the boy's story on March 17, 1916. He told the interrogators that he was the boy who held Pablo Lope's horse. Pablo was Villa's second in command. The paper reported the interrogation:

> Twice as he talked he asked for a book that he always keeps with him and reads whenever he can. It is a story of India and is called *A Fallen Idol*. As the shadows lengthened the little bandit spoke only in soft short sentences, the morphine was doing its work, he was almost asleep, but he roused himself and said, "Me bueno muchacho" (I am a good boy.) He was asleep. Pancho Villa has very, very much to answer for to his God.

As the Villistas retreated, Major Frank Tompkins mounted up two troops of cavalry and chased after them. He kept up a running fight, crossing the border and venturing fifteen miles into Mexican land. Major Tompkins's troops did severe damage to the Villistas. Seventy-five bandits were reported killed, and more wounded. The major's troops suffered no losses. Pancho Villa's bandits were badly beaten, scattered, and on the run. Unfortunately, the cavalry had to return to New Mexico Territory when they ran out of ammunition. Nevertheless, it was an exhausted and triumphant troop that rode into Columbus.

The United States would not let Villa's bandito raid go unpunished. Five days after the attack, General "Black Jack" Pershing organized a punitive expedition using the 7th, 10th, and 13th Cavalry Regiments. Also under his command was the aviation section of the Signal Corps. The squadron had eight outdated airplanes that were underpowered and weighted down with armor plate. Only three were armed. Their commander was Captain Benjamin, who had learned his craft from Orville Wright. Also assigned to Pershing were several motorized vehicles, including some that were the forerunner of the modern tank.

Mule trains carried fuel for the motorized vehicles. Motor vehicles were so new to the army that there were no experienced drivers. Accustomed to urging on their mounts and pack animals, the inexperienced drivers cried to their vehicles with yells of "whoa" and "giddyup." The "flying machines" and motorized vehicles proved to have many problems and were not effective in the desert.

Pershing's troops eventually traveled 1,400 miles into Mexican territory. They were engaged in several skirmishes, but never found Villa. After eleven months, the punitive action was called off.

But Villa's bandit gang had been destroyed, and he was never again a major threat. The failed Columbus raid was his last chance for glory. In 1923 Pancho Villa was assassinated in Parral, Mexico; and his body, beheaded.

Ironically, the punitive expedition that the raid prompted was the last hurrah for the mounted cavalry, their last chance for glory. Lessons learned with the motorized vehicles and "flying machines" led to their successful use in World War I, when the roar of engines replaced the sound of hoofbeats forever.

The true motivation for Villa's attack has never been determined. Certainly Villa wanted to gain the attention and respect of his people at a time when his country was in turmoil and its leadership undetermined. Glory was another possible goal. In addition, if Villa had been cheated of the arms he purchased from Sam Ravel, revenge could have been another reason for the attack. But there is no proof he actually purchased merchandise from Ravel; it is more likely he was hoping to secure more arms and money by robbing the store. Although he had many men, some with military rank, his group lacked the discipline, the leadership, the recognition, and the formal structure of an army. They were a large number of bandits brought together with promises of riches and dreams and personal gain. Their attack on a small town was unprovoked, not driven by international politics, and amounted to nothing more than a large outlaw raid. Villa is still considered the Mexican outlaw who raided a town.

Bibliography

General

Hertzog, Peter. *Outlaws of New Mexico*. Santa Fe: Sunstone Press, 1984.

Nash, Jay Robert. *Encyclopedia of Western Lawmen & Outlaws*. New York: Da Capo Press, 1994.

O'Neal, Bill. *Encyclopedia of Western Gunfighters*. Norman: University of Oklahoma, 1979.

Robert "Clay" Allison

Bryan, Howard. *Robbers, Rogues and Ruffians: True Tales of the Wild West in New Mexico*. Santa Fe: Clear Light Publishers, 1991.

Cleaveland, Agnes Morley. *No Life for a Lady*. Lincoln: University of Nebraska Press, 1977.

Hogan, Ray. *The Life and Death of Clay Allison*. New York: New American Library, 1961.

L'Aloge, Bob. *The Incident of New Mexico's Nightriders: A True Account of the Socorro Vigilantes*. Sunnyside, WA: BJS Brand Books, 1992.

Parsons, Chuck. *Clay Allison: Portrait of a Shootist*. Seagraves, TX: Pioneer Book Publishers, 1983.

Trachtman, Paul. *The Old West: The Gunfighters*. New York: Time-Life Books, 1976.

Truett, John A. *Clay Allison: Legend of Cimarron*. Santa Fe: Sunstone Press, 1998.

Jesse Evans

Bartholomew, Ed. *Jesse Evans: A Texas Hide-Burner.* Houston: Frontier Press of Texas, 1955.

Hough, Emerson. *The Story of the Outlaw: A Study of the Western Desperado.* New York: Copper Square Press, 2001.

Jacobsen, Joel. *Such Men as Billy the Kid: The Lincoln County War Reconsidered.* Lincoln and Norman: University of Nebraska Press, 1994.

L'Aloge, Bob. *The Code of the West.* Las Cruces: B & J Publications, 1992.

————. *Knights of the Sixgun: A Diary of Gunfighters, Outlaws and Villains of New Mexico.* Las Cruces: Yucca Tree Press, 1993.

McCright, Grady E., and James H. Powell. *Jesse Evans: Lincoln County Badman.* College Station, TX: Early West Series, Creative Publishing Co., 1983.

"Mysterious" Dave Mather

Bryan, Howard. *Robbers, Rogues and Ruffians: True Tales of the Wild West.* Santa Fe: Clear Light Publishers, 1991.

————. *Wildest of the Wild West: True Tales of a Frontier Town on the Santa Fe Trail.* Santa Fe: Clear Light Publishers, 1988.

L'Aloge, Bob. *The Code of the West.* Las Cruces: B & J Publications, 1992.

"The Dodge City Gang, of Las Vegas, NM." www.legendsofamerica .com/WE-DodgeCityGang2.html.

Metz, Leon Claire. *The Shooters.* New York: Berkley Books, 1976.

"Old West Legends: Mysterious Dave Mather—Lawman or Outlaw?" www.legendsofamerica.com/WE-DaveMather.html.

The Stockton Gang

125th Anniversary of the Death of Porter Stockton. *Aztec Museum Association Newsletter*, Vol. XXIX, January 1, 2006.

Beckner, Raymond R. *Guns along the Silvery San Juan.* Carson City: Master Printers, 1975.

Jacobsen, Joel. *Such Men as Billy the Kid: The Lincoln County War Reconsidered.* Lincoln and London: University of Nebraska, 1994.

Thompson, Jonathan. "Midnight Murder." *Silverton Standard & The Miner,* 2003.

"Dirty" Dave Raudabaugh

Bryan, Howard. *Robbers, Rogues and Ruffians: True Tales of the Wild West.* Santa Fe: Clear Light Publishers, 1991.

————. *Wildest of the Wild West: True Tales of a Frontier Town on the Santa Fe Trail.* Santa Fe: Clear Light Publishers, 1988.

"Chronology of the Life of Billy the Kid and the Lincoln County War." www.angelfire.com/mi2/billythekid/chronology.html.

Fulton, Maurice G. *History of the Lincoln County War: A Classic Account of Billy the Kid.* Tucson: The University of Arizona Press, 1968.

Hough, Emerson. *The Story of the Outlaw: A Study of the Western Desperado.* New York: Cooper Square Press, 2001.

L'Aloge, Bob. *The Incident of New Mexico's Nightriders: A True Account of the Socorro Vigilantes.* Sunnyside: BJS Brand Books, 1992.

Rickards, Colin. *Mysterious Dave Mather.* Santa Fe: The Blue Feather Press, 1968.

Stanley, F. *Desperadoes of New Mexico*. Denver: World Press, Inc., 1953.

Milton Yarberry

Basso, Matthew, Laura McCall, and Dee Garceau, editors. *Across the Great Divide: Cultures of Manhood in the American West*. New York: Routledge, 2001.

Bryan, Howard. *Robbers, Rogues and Ruffians: True Tales of the Wild West in New Mexico*. Santa Fe: Clear Light Publishers, 1991.

DeArment, Robert K. *Deadly Dozen: Twelve Forgotten Gunfighters of the Old West*. Norman: University of Oklahoma Press, 2003.

L'Aloge, Bob. *The Code of the West*. Las Cruces: B & J Publications, 1992.

————. *Riders Along the Rio Grande*. Las Cruces: RCS Press, 1992.

Simmons, Marc. *When Six-Guns Ruled: Outlaw Tales of the Southwest*. Santa Fe: Ancient City Press, 1990.

Billy the Kid

Bartholomew, Ed. *Jesse Evans: A Texas Hide-Burner*. Houston: Frontier Press of Texas, 1955.

Bryan, Howard. *Robbers, Rogues, and Ruffians: True Tales of the Wild West*. Santa Fe: Clear Light Publishers, 1991.

————. *Wildest of the Wild West: True Tales of a Frontier Town on the Santa Fe Trail*. Santa Fe: Clear Light Publishers, 1988.

"Chronology of the Life of Billy the Kid and the Lincoln County War." www.angelfire.com/mi2/billythekid/chronology.html.

"The Death of Billy the Kid, 1881." www.eyewitnesstohistory.com/billythekid.htm.

Fulton, Maurice G. *History of the Lincoln County War: A Classic Account of Billy the Kid.* Tucson: The University of Arizona Press, 1997.

Hough, Emerson. *The Story of the Outlaw: A Study of the Western Desperado.* New York: Cooper Square Press, 2001.

L'Aloge, Bob. *The Code of the West.* Las Cruces: Yucca Tree Press, 1992.

————. *The Incident of New Mexico's Nightriders: A True Account of the Socorro Vigilantes.* Sunnyside: BJS Brand Books, 1992.

————. *Knights of the Sixgun: A Diary of Gunfighters, Outlaws and Villains of New Mexico.* Las Cruces: Yucca Tree Press, 1991.

————. *Riders along the Rio Grande: A Collection of Outlaws, Prostitutes & Vigilantes.* Las Cruces: RCS Press, 1992.

Metz, Leon Claire. *The Shooters.* New York: Berkley Books, 1976.

Myers, Amanda Lee. "2 digging for Billy the Kid face legal woes." *Arizona Daily Star,* Sunday, May 14, 2006.

"Pioneer Oral History." Center for Southwest Research, Collection MSS 123 BC, Transcripts 22, 113, 123. Universities Libraries, The University of New Mexico.

Sharp, Jay W. "The Night Pat Garrett (Probably) Shot Billy the Kid." www.desertusa.com/mag04/july/billy.html.

Simmons, Marc. *When Six-Guns Ruled.* Santa Fe: Ancient City Press, 1990.

Trachtman, Paul. *The Old West: The Gunfighters*. New York: Time-Life Books, 1974.

Joel Fowler

Bryan, Howard. *Robbers, Rogues and Ruffians: True Tales of the Wild West in New Mexico*. Santa Fe: Clear Light Publishers, 1991.

Hough, Emerson. *The Story of the Outlaw: A Study of the Western Desperado*. New York: First Cooper Square Press, 2001.

L'Aloge, Bob. *The Incident of New Mexico's Nightriders: A True Account of the Socorro Vigilantes*. Sunnyside: BJS Brand Books, 1992.

"Pioneer Oral History." Center for Southwest Research, Collection MSS 123 BC, Transcripts 336, 345, 346, 352. University Libraries, The University of New Mexico.

Simmons, Marc. *When Six-Guns Ruled: Outlaw Tales of the Southwest*. Santa Fe: Ancient City Press, 1990.

Ada Hulmes

"Ada Hume, who achieved somewhat of a reputation here a few years ago for killing her man, is now a variety actress at Creede, Colorado." *Southwest Sentinel*, April 8, 1892.

Bullis, Don. "Silver City: Wild and Woolly." *Rancho Observer*, October 23, 2003.

"Grant is the only county in the Territory which has as yet sent a woman to the Santa Fe penitentiary." *Southwest Sentinel*, October 25, 1889.

Tanner, Karen Holliday, and John D. Tanner Jr. "Murder and Scandal in New Mexico: The Case of Ada Hulmes." *Wild West*, September 2003.

Vincent Silva

Bryan, Howard. *Wildest of the Wild West: True Tales of a Frontier Town on the Santa Fe Trail*. Santa Fe: Clear Light Publishers, 1988.

L'Aloge, Bob. *The Code of the West*. Las Cruces: Yucca Tree Press, 1992.

McGrath, Tom. *Vincent Silva and His Forty Thieves*. Las Vegas: Fray Angélico Chávez History Library, 1960.

Simmons, Marc. *When Six-Guns Ruled*. Santa Fe: Ancient City Press, 1990.

"The Worst Outlaw." *Santa Fe Reporter*, August 13, 1981, p. 19.

De Baca, Carlos. C., *Vincent Silva: New Mexico's Vice King of the Nineties*, Smith-Hursch Las Vegas, NM, 1938.

Stanley, F. *Desperados of New Mexico*. Denver: World Press, 1953.

Therp, N. Howard. *Bandits of New Mexico*. Santa Fe: Fray Angelico Chavez History Library.

Thomas Edward "Black Jack" Ketchum and His Gang

"Black Jack and Gang." *The Florence Tribune*, January 16, 1897.

"Swing Into Eternity, Thomas Ketchum, the Famous Bandit Died Game." *The Clayton Enterprise*, April 30, 1901.

L'Aloge, Bob. *The Incident of New Mexico's Nightriders: A True Account of the Socorro Vigilantes*. Sunnyside: BJS Brand Books, 1992.

"Pioneer Oral History." Center for Southwest Research, Collection MSS 123BC, Transcripts 22, 113, 114, 123, 175, 357. University Libraries, The University of New Mexico.

Simmons, Marc. *When Six-Guns Ruled: Outlaw Tales of the Southwest.* Santa Fe: Ancient City Press, 1990.

Spradley, Berry. *Ketchum Genealogy.* Clayton, NM. Union County Historical Society, 1986.

Pancho Villa's Last Chance for Glory

Askins, Charles. *Gunfighters.* Washington: National Rifle Association of America, 1981.

Dean, Richard R. *The Columbus Story.* Columbus, NM: Friends of Pancho Villa State Park, 1991.

"Pancho Villa's Columbus Raid." Oral history videotape, Pancho Villa State Park, Columbus, NM.

"Prisoners Here from Columbus." *The Deming Headlight,* March 17, 1916.

Wallace, Andrew. "The Sabre Retires: Pershing's Cavalry Campaign in Mexico, 1916." Tucson, *The Smoke Signal,* Tucson Corral of the Westerners, Spring 1964, no. 9.

Yockelson, Mitchell. *The United States Armed Forces and the Mexican Punitive Expedition: Part 1 & 2.* Washington, The U.S. National Archives & Records Administration. September 2, 2006.

About the Author

Barbara Marriott has a PhD in cultural anthropology, a thirst for knowledge, and an insatiable curiosity, giving her the enthusiasm and the tools to research, analyze, and weave together stories of people, cultures, and events.

In the past three years, Barbara has written three nonfiction history books. Two of them, *Annie's Guests* and *Canyon of Gold*, are books on the Old West. She lives in Tucson, Arizona.